# Instructor's Manual

# Writer's Mind

# Instructor's Manual

# Writer's Mind
## Crafting Fiction

**Richard Cohen**

NTC *Publishing Group*
Lincolnwood, Illinois USA

Published by NTC Publishing Group, 4255 West Touhy Avenue,
Lincolnwood (Chicago), Illinois 60646-1975 U.S.A.
4 5 6 7 8 9 0 VP 9 8 7 6 5 4 3 2 1

# CONTENTS

# The Idea of This Book

*Writer's mind* is this book's phrase for the way writers see the world. Writer's mind is an outlook, a frame of reference, and a way of being. It is a self-discipline and a way of responding to both success and failure. There may or may not be such a thing as a typical writer's personality, but most writers share a kind of family resemblance stemming from the simple fact that at every moment of their lives they are looking for material to write about and for ways to write better. Everything that happens to a writer happens on two levels: the level of ordinary human experience and the level of potential literary material. Thus even the most tragic events are redeemed for a constructive use; writing creates a purpose for suffering, whether or not such a purpose existed beforehand. Writers tend to see everything, even their own griefs, with a certain detachment, assessing every experience for how it will play in print. Writers also share a commitment to their craft, to their language, and to the primacy of personal vision over external demands. No matter what the particulars of the vision, each writer can recognize the presence—or absence—of that commitment in another.

The above points aren't explicitly emphasized in the student edition, but rather underlie it as assumptions. The book attempts to convey *writer's mind* by example: showing it as well as telling it. There's a good deal of discussion of such matters as self-discipline, work habits, and the process of literary invention, but the outlook of *writer's mind* is also intended to be present in the book's tone throughout. The book is the product of one writer's mind, and its voice is unswervingly personal: at times irreverent, at times self-revealing, at times sardonic, at times quirky. Such a voice says, in effect, "This is what it's like to be a writer. This is how writers really think, act, view the world. You don't have to think, act, or view the world the way this particular writer does; what's important is that you think, act, view the world in some way that's authentically your own."

In recent years a great deal of lip service has been given to the personal element in student writing: to developing the students' literary voices and getting them to write about what's meaningful to them. Oddly, however, the books that teach this lesson are usually written in a rather impersonal style—doubtless because they're too conscious of being aimed at educators. As the saying goes, they talk the talk but they don't walk the walk—they don't practice what they preach. *Writer's Mind* tries to encourage personal writing in students by *being* personal writing.

At the same time, it delivers more practical advice on craftsmanship than writers' manuals that take a purely nuts and bolts approach. Plot, characterization, style, theme, drafting, revision, and numerous other topics are explored from the standpoint of a writer's career-long, daily knowledge. The approach to any given topic is a wide-angle one. The book attempts to spell out as many specific methods as possible but doesn't attempt to establish an orthodox technique. The message is not, "Do it this way, not that way." The message is, "Writers have written in these various ways, among which the author of this book favors one way. Try them all out and see which you prefer."

1

In other words, *Writer's Mind* combines approaches that are generally found in two different kinds of books on writing: the practical and the inspirational. There are many practical handbooks of fiction writing on the market, but their overall impact is numbingly formulaic; after reading them, one could not hope to produce more than a rudimentary, competent piece of hackwork. There are also inspirational volumes on writing, which generally emphasize freeing the creative imagination, doing visualization exercises, keeping journals, and so on—what a cynic might call "touchy-feely." Such exercises can be genuinely valuable, but those books generally have little if any practical advice to offer on the craft of fiction writing, and they tend to be wildly, gushily optimistic about the psychological benefits of spending one's free time scribbling in a notebook. After reading them, one might hope to write an admirably descriptive personal letter or diary entry.

*Writer's Mind* tries to be as practically informative as the first type of writer's manual and as inspiring as the second, without succumbing to the flaws of either—without recommending formulas and without touting writing as a pastel-colored paradise, a therapeutic panacea. Its inspiration is in its realism. It doesn't flinch from discussing the inevitable frustrations of a writing life, but it presents that kind of life as supremely worthwhile for those who feel called to it. Not everyone feels called to it, of course. Implicitly, the book is a lesson in how to listen for the call.

In its quest for a realistic vision of writing, the book does something else important: it examines the conventional wisdom of the field and, in some cases, debunks it. Creative writing students in America today are subjected to a good many buzzwords, platitudes, and half-truths, dressed up as eternal verities. "Write what you know," "Find your own voice," and "Show, don't tell" are three of the most obvious. But what do they really mean, and how true are they? When are they useful, and what are their limitations? *Writer's Mind* tries to question received ideas in a critical, original way. As with the topics of craftsmanship, the message here is not, "Do this, don't do that," but "Some writers have said this; what does it mean; and what do you think?"

After reading *Writer's Mind*, one might hope to write a serious work of literature.

## How to Use the Book in a Course

Readers who purchase this book from a bookstore or check it out of a library will read it in private, from front to back, and that time-honored method can be used in a course as well. You can simply assign the book at the beginning of the course with a recommendation that students finish it by the end of the course or by a stated deadline, such as after three or four weeks.

On the other hand, depending on your student's grade level and your own teaching style, you may want to assign the book in smaller chunks at stated points over the course of a term or a year. The most obvious way to do so is to parcel out the chapters week by week, or class meeting by class meeting, from the beginning of the book to the end. Here is a suggested schedule, based on a sixteen-week semester:

Week   1:   Chapters 1–3 (introduction to the nature of stories and subjects)

Week   2:   Chapter 4 (plot)

Week   3:   Chapter 5 (characterization)

Week   4:   Chapter 5 (characterization, continued)

Week   5:   Chapter 6 (dialogue)

Week   6:   Chapter 7 (description)

Week   7:   Chapter 8 (modes of narration)

Week   8:   Chapter 9 (point of view and narrative distance)

Week   9:   Chapter 10 (style, voice, and tone)

Week  10:   Chapters 11 and 12 (theme and experimentation in fiction)

Week  11:   Chapter 13 (prewriting: inventing and developing ideas)

Week  12:   Chapter 14 (drafting)

Week  13:   Chapter 15 (revision)

Week  14:   Chapters 15 and 16 (revision, continued, and work habits)

Week  15:   Chapters 17–19 (audience, education, careers)

Week  16:   Chapters 20 and 21 (getting published; the writer's life)

Depending on the number of weeks in your course and on your personal ideas about writing, you're encouraged to vary this scheme in whatever way suits you, expanding or contracting the amount of time devoted to specific topics. Notice that in the above schedule, Chapters 1–3 and 16–21 are compressed into more than one chapter per week, while Chapters 4–15 get at least one full week per chapter and sometimes two weeks. Those middle chapters are the "core" of the course in terms of the pragmatic craft of writing. Chapters 1–3 are a broad overview of what writing is, what stories are, and where stories come from, and they can be discussed together in a single session, although the ideas introduced in those chapters will resonate throughout the book. Chapters 16–21, meanwhile, deal with matters of career rather than craft. Depending on your judgment of your students' interest and readiness, you might give these topics the relatively full discussion outlined above, or you may want to compress them even further, perhaps omitting some of them entirely (with a recommendation that interested students read them on their own).

The above schedule assumes that you're teaching a course in fiction. However, in high school English and in freshman composition, you're likely to be covering several other major forms of writing, with fiction reserved for a single unit of the course. In that case, you might want to cover Chapters 13–15 at the beginning of the course, because their focus on prewriting, drafting, and revising can be applied to any kind of writing. Then, when you return to fiction at some later point, you might concentrate on the core craftsmanship chapters, 4–10. Chapters 11 and 12 also treat topics of craftsmanship, but ones that are less indispensable in the context of a survey course. Chapters 1–3, the introductory discussion of the nature of stories, provide a useful starting point for your fiction unit but can be jettisoned if you're pressed for time. Chapters 16–21 can be reserved for the end of the course if you have some time left over; you might want to summarize these concluding topics briefly and ask students which ones they're most interested in discussing.

Whatever schedule you use, you may want to assess students' reading informally in discussion, but it's not recommended that you give a formal test on the book as a component of students' final grades. Formal assessment should be based on their writing and their in-class contributions. (See "Assessment," on page 5 of this manual.)

## How to Use the Exercises

At the end of each chapter of the student edition, there are at least two exercises (usually more), at least one of which is directed toward cooperative learning. In each chapter's section of this manual, there are at least two more exercises under the straightforward heading "More Exercises." Altogether the student edition contains about a hundred exercises and this manual about a hundred more. The exercises are of many kinds. Some propose ideas or starting points for short stories. Others are technique exercises that work on specific skills such as description or dialogue. Others trigger discussion. Others are thought exercises, intended to help students plan their projects or visualize their possible future as writers. Others propose longer-term projects, a handful of which point the way to a potential life's work. Some are a mixture of types, and most can be used as entryways into discussion of the topics treated in the given chapters. The exercises are not labeled by type, and there is no intended difference between the type or quality of exercises in the student edition and the type or quality of exercises in this manual. The manual simply gives you more exercises than there was room for in the student edition.

This is important: These exercises are not intended to be an extra burden on either the instructor or the student. An instructor may decide not to have students do any of the exercises as part of the formal course work. Other instructors will pick and choose. (It would be impossible, for reasons of time, for any class to do all the exercises.) It is entirely appropriate—and perhaps quite pragmatic—to view all the exercises as thought exercises; students can benefit from thinking about them imaginatively, without necessarily having to write them out.

At the beginning of the course, you might want to commend the exercises to your students with the words, "Take a look at the exercises and if you find any that you think you might want to do, do them." And the author says the same thing to you, the instructor. If you feel that one or more of the exercises will be particularly useful in helping students work out some of their writing problems, by all means assign those exercises either to the individual students, to a small group, or to the whole class. Or—more enjoyably—recommend the assignments without assigning them. Perhaps one of the most rewarding uses of the exercises will be to match a particular exercise to a student who can benefit from it: to recognize a student's need for work on description, for instance, and to suggest just the right bit of practice that will build up that student's mastery.

Some instructors, including the author, like to have students write in-class exercises, especially at the beginnings of class sessions, especially at the beginning of the course. If you favor in-class writing, look over each chapter's exercises before beginning the study of that chapter, and mark the exercises you feel will work best during the time you allot for such writing.

It is recommended that you give students a lot of leeway to interpret the exercises as they see fit—indeed, that you encourage them to alter the assignments creatively whenever they come up with new ideas. The intent is to stimulate students' flow of invention, not to test their ability to follow directions. "Coloring outside the lines" is highly approved of, and talented students will certainly be able to think up exercises of their own. If an exercise says, for instance, "Write a story about a character who starts out unsympathetic and ends up sympathetic," it's okay if a student decides to do the opposite. Do talk to the student about the alterations, though, to make sure that the effects achieved are those intended. If the student wanted to write about a character who started out unsympathetic and ended up sympathetic, but the written draft produced the opposite effect, that would be important to discuss! For this reason, you might ask students to append a brief note at the beginning or end of any written exercise whose directions they've altered.

A further condition to ensure that the exercises remain enjoyable and helpful: Don't assess them formally! Don't even think about grading them! (See "Assessment," below.)

## Assessment

At its autumn, 1993 meeting, the National Council of Teachers of English (NCTE) passed a resolution declaring that formal assessment in creative writing courses be kept to a minimum. This most welcome and intelligent decision relieves the author of the burden of making a sustained argument against formal assessment at this point.

Few teachers have worked with students' fiction without feeling that a formal grade was beside the point. We can't know that Jenny is a better writer than Jerry in the same way that we can know that Jenny is better at solving geometry problems than Jerry. We may discern, almost instantly, that Jenny's spelling and grammar are better, but that says nothing about the relative strengths of the students' imaginations or—and this is extremely important—about their potential to grow as writers after they leave the course. (Whether creative writing instructors should correct and grade grammar, spelling, and other mechanical matters is a much-debated issue. This author feels that in upper-level courses, these matters are beneath the instructor's notice and a drain on the instructor's time. Some instructors, however, feel that mechanics is one area of writing in which they can actually produce a tangible improvement in students' work. The lower the grade level at which you're teaching, the more likely that you're teaching an integrated curriculum in which correction and grading of mechanics is appropriate.)

Encouraging talented writers to keep writing should be one major purpose of grading. That's one reason why overassessment is so dangerous: A low grade to a student who secretly yearns to write, but whose talent hasn't happened to catch your eye yet, can be tremendously damaging to the student's self-esteem. Talent in youngsters is often hard to uncover beneath its layers of disguise, and the most obvious cases are not necessarily the ones that will flourish through adulthood. Even adult readers' opinions of great writers vary widely. For example, Vladimir Nabokov, in his lectures on Russian literature at Cornell University in the 1950s, gave an "A+" to Tolstoy, an "A" to Chekhov, an "A-" to Turgenev—and a "D" to Dostoyevsky. It was funny in the lectures, but what if as a student Dostoyevsky really had gotten a "D," just because the teacher had a blind spot? And we all have blind spots.

The opposite case—giving an unexpectedly high grade to a student who previously had not thought of himself or herself as talented—can make a wonderful difference in a young writer's development, but the same effect can be obtained, more convincingly, by talking to the student about the writing and encouraging him or her to keep at it.

In a perfect world, therefore, creative writing courses would be pass-fail, with failures resulting only from refusal to do the work. In the real world, of course, we must give grades. How to do so without being unfair to some students? Some pointers, which you may or may not agree with:

1.  Give as few grades as possible per student per course. As stated previously, don't grade writing exercises, comprehension of this book, or other reading (e.g., published fiction). If you feel comfortable doing so, refrain from grading students' individual short stories; give discursive evaluations instead. How can we honestly say, "This is a 'B' story, and that one's an 'A'?" If possible, the end-of-course grade should be the only grade the student receives, especially after the first year of college.

2.  Use conferences to give students an interim idea of how they're doing. Give plenty of feedback, and ask students to tell you their own impressions of how they're doing, too, so that you can correct any misconceptions on their parts. It's okay to give students fairly precise ideas of what grade they're working toward, for instance, "If you keep up the good work you're doing, you'll probably end up with around a 'B+' for this course." But try to reinforce the idea that grades in creative writing are often something of a compromise and can never accurately convey the living quality of a writer's work. Ideally, you should hold one conference per story per student, plus a final portfolio conference. One conference per student per term is an absolute minimum.

3.  At the end of the course, grade the student's entire portfolio as whole. The portfolio might include not only the student's own writing, but copies of all classmates' work on which the student has written comments. The portfolio grade will be the single most important component of the student's course grade. Hold a portfolio conference with each student separately in the final week or so of the course, giving the student a chance to agree with or dissent from your evaluation of the portfolio.

4.  The perennial question in this field is, "Should we grade students for talent or for effort?" The answer, of course, is "Both." And the proportions might vary

from student to student. A student with little talent who tries hard, whose writing improves, and who contributes to discussions may very well deserve an "A." On the other hand, a student who writes a brilliant story but clams up in class may also deserve an "A." Two very different kinds of student, one common denominator: their presence enhances the class. (The student who contributes in both ways, of course, deserves the highest grade.)

More and more creative writing instructors have begun counting class participation in students' grades. It makes a lot of sense. Your aim, in large part, is to turn your classroom into a thriving writers' workshop, and students who participate in discussions help you do so. Talking about other students' stories, or about one's own, is also something that can be done by all students regardless of talent; it's a leveling factor. If you decide to include class participation in your grade, tell students so during the first meeting of the course, and specify the percentage of the final grade thus covered (it usually ranges from 25 percent to 50 percent).

Some instructors also count attendance as part of the final grade, particularly in upper-level college courses where students are prone not to attend. This alleviates the nonattendance problem and, again, provides an objective variable for grading. If you adopt this tactic, make sure to announce the fact during the first meeting. Then take attendance at all subsequent meetings. The percentage of the grade devoted to attendance usually ranges from 10 percent to 25 percent. Alternatively, some instructors use attendance as a grade determinant in borderline cases, tipping the scale up or down. Some instructors state a policy of grading down a set amount for absences: for example, deducting half a grade for every two unexcused absences.

Grading for class participation creates the problem of how to get students to participate. Many writers, after all, are introverted. The knowledge that class participation affects their grade will certainly be one incentive for them to talk. Here's another: Whenever the class discusses a student's story, assign one student (not the writer of the story, of course) to lead the discussion. This student will need to do an especially careful job of reading the story and should write half a page or a page of comments about it. The student begins discussion of the story by giving a brief talk based on his or her notes. Then, the student opens the discussion up to the class and acts as moderator, calling on other participants and adding expert comments whenever he or she sees fit. (The writer of the story is free to respond to any comments by classmates; this too provides a mechanism for quiet students to participate.) You may wish to use the student's performance as discussion leader as a stated percentage of the class participation grade. Each student should get at least one chance to be a discussion leader during the course.

5.   Here's a grading tip the author learned from Laurence Goldstein at the University of Michigan: During the final class meeting, perhaps in conjunction with their filling out evaluations of you, have each student write down a grade

for each member of the class, including himself or herself. (You might wish to pass around class rosters for the purpose.) Encourage students to add one or two sentences commenting on their grading decisions. You, of course, are not under the slightest obligation to agree with these peer gradings, and you must tell students so, but peer grading might provide you with some insights and lead you to appreciate overlooked aspects of some students' work. (For instance, instructors are not always aware of which students provide their classmates with the most useful feedback on stories.) Students' self-gradings can be surprisingly enlightening if taken with the appropriate measure of salt.

## Some Thoughts on Teaching Writing

It's a truism among creative writing instructors that the less the instructor *seems* to do, the better the class is going. Good creative writing classes, most of the time, are discussion groups that carry themselves by their own momentum. The instructor's job is to establish the momentum by creating a favorable climate in the first few meetings. In later meetings, his or her role often becomes that of a moderator, umpire, insightful oracle, traffic manager, and authority on etiquette. If the students keep talking and the discussion remains civil, you're doing well.

This was borne home to the author once when he chanced to oversleep a class—no small accomplishment, since the section met at one in the afternoon. Returning the next week to mumble his apologies, the author learned to his amazement that the students had not fled the classroom in his absence. They had held a two-hour workshop as usual. The scheduled stories were discussed, the student experts led the discussion well, and volunteers signed up for the next week's discussion. The class rhythm had been established so smoothly by that point (about two-thirds of the way through the semester) that the instructor was no longer needed. It was the ultimate triumph of pedagogy! However, as they say, "Do not try this at home."

How does one establish a smooth, self-sustaining rhythm of class participation? It begins with small things at the first meeting or two. The first thing you do, probably, will be to introduce yourself and your course requirements. Present yourself as a human being with a personality; tell a little about your background, your education, your teaching and writing experience, your tastes in literature. Be clear, explicit, and upbeat about all course requirements: how many stories you'll be assigning, what the readings will be, and so on. Hand out a printed syllabus if you have one.

One of your ongoing tasks as a creative writing teacher, beginning with first impressions and lasting over the length of your career, is to establish a persona—perhaps one that's authoritative and knowledgeable but friendly, patient, relaxed, and quirky to the extent that any writer (even a teacher!) is allowed to be. This doesn't mean you're supposed to become buddies with your students; on the contrary, the most effective instructors often take care to maintain a certain distance. The situation is somewhat analogous to that of a therapist: You demonstrate that you're sympathetic and available for consultations, but you only reveal things about yourself that serve an appropriate, professional, helping function. And as a teacher, of course, you're *not* a therapist and should resist going as deep into a student's personal problems as a therapist would. There's a tendency for creative writing students to turn to their instructors for help in dealing with their personal turmoil, but the upshot can be that student and instructor alike flounder. Better to steer the student gently toward professional counseling.

At the first meeting, it's also customary to ask students to introduce themselves. Many instructors like to go around the room, giving each student a turn to say his or her name and anything else the students wish to, such as a couple of sentences about what kind of writing they hope to do, what kind of books they like to read, what their background is, and the like. You might propose a topic or question that each student will briefly answer, such as, "Name a book you've read recently and briefly tell us what you liked or disliked about it," or, "Name your favorite writer," or, "How much experience have you had taking creative writing courses?" Students can be allowed to pass, but they must at least state their names and state that they pass.

This very simple exercise automatically starts a class discussion in which every student has participated. You may either turn to something else once every student has been introduced or pick up a topic that was broached in the introductions and continue the discussion. You might go on to describe your own teaching style and your expectations/hopes for the course, or you might ask students what their vision of a good creative writing course—and of good writing—is. This would be a good point at which to discuss Chapters 1–3.

The first couple of weeks tend to be the most awkward in a creative writing class, because students have not yet "primed the pump" by turning in their first short stories. These weeks, therefore, provide good opportunities to discuss literature, to study this book, or to do in-class writing (either short exercises or students' stories). If you're having the students write short exercises, encourage volunteers to read theirs aloud. Alternatively, you might collect all the exercises and read them aloud at random, anonymously. That will keep students from being embarrassed by their rough efforts. You might do the exercise yourself and include your own paper anonymously. However, it is recommended that you *never* distribute a completed, unpublished story of your own to the class for discussion. As many instructors over the years have found, the students' response is almost invariably a blow to the ego—ranging from total silence to the question once asked of the author, "That was a joke, wasn't it?"

You'll also need, at the first meeting, to give students a schedule of assignment deadlines. This is a perennial sticking point in creative writing classes; every instructor has his or her own method, and no method has been found to be perfect. Should you assign three stories per semester or four? Should you assign a required number of pages, such as forty per semester? Should you have every student submit a story at the same time or stagger the schedule? Should you have students submit one copy of each story or two copies (one for you and one to return to them) or one copy per class member plus one for you? How should stories be distributed among the students—by photocopy, by reading aloud, or both? Should you have students give you their stories at the end of a class period, or should you provide a box outside your office in which they can put the stories at any time during a given week? Should every story that every student writes be distributed to the whole class, or should each student be given the option of distributing, let's say, his or her choice of two out of four stories, or should you take it upon yourself to distribute only those stories you like best?

You'll have to work these questions out for yourself, and you'll probably adjust your methods during the course of your teaching career. The author, having tried a staggered schedule of student submissions, with volunteers signing up over a period of three weeks, later came to believe it was better to have all students hand in their stories at the same time. The instructor can then decide which group of stories will be discussed during which class meetings—perhaps at the rate of two per hour. Having students submit enough copies for the entire class has turned out to be a good strategy, the only drawback being that the instructor and each student then receives, say, fifteen or twenty stories at a time. Over the next two or three or four weeks, students will then bring to class, from among that master group of stories, the handful of stories to be discussed at any given meeting. It's your responsibility to remind students of which stories will be dealt with at the next meeting; you might hand out a written schedule, or write the names on the board, or say them aloud and have students keep notes. At the session during which a given story is discussed, all students should bring in their copies of that story, with their own handwritten comments; at the end of class, all students should return the story to its writer. Thus the writer has fifteen or twenty copies of the story with feedback. The writer may want to review those comments when the time comes to revise the story—but it should not be a requirement that the writer agree with, and obey, his or her readers' comments! Near the end of the course, when you're amassing portfolios (perhaps the next-to-last meeting), each student will then return each copy of each story to the student reader whose comments are on that copy. This allows you to gauge the quality of each student's responses to his or her peers' work as part of the portfolio grade.

The logistics can be complicated and confusing, in short, but once you've established a workable system for yourself, you'll feel comfortable and you'll be able to use it repeatedly—as long as you accept the fact that no system is perfect!

At the same time the class members return their copies and comments to the writer of a story, you too will do so. Your comments, of course, will be the ones that have the greatest weight. And all students, not just the writer, will want to know what you think about each story. The class may be able to run itself in terms of quantity of discussion, but the instructor has a crucial role in the quality of discussion. When the students have said what they have to say about a story (and you may in some cases want to cut off discussion if you find it becoming repetitious, irrelevant, or destructive), there will inevitably be points you wanted to raise that they themselves did not raise. Your own comments can serve as the wrap-up to the discussion of each story, after which the class proceeds to the next story or to dismissal. One good way to wrap things up is to read aloud or paraphrase aloud your written comments about the story and then add any observations or insights that occurred to you during the discussion (some of which you may have added to your written comments). These comments, of course, won't necessarily be limited to the specific story at hand; they may be about some ongoing technical question that has come up repeatedly in class and that the story exemplifies, or about writing in general, or about literature or life.

This section has described a smoothly running, cohesive, cordial, voluble classroom, and that's a fairly realistic description of many creative writing classrooms. Given a chance, students tend to enjoy creative writing—to look upon it as a fun course. It's a place where they can express themselves, laugh, broach their feelings (veiled as fiction—or not), talk about things that matter to them, and feel that the pedagogical authority is actually on their side for once. Students probably make more good friends in creative writing courses than in most other subjects.

There are two major dangers to this user-friendly approach. One is that class discussions will be dominated by a very few students who talk all the time, while others retreat into the background. The solution is to let students know that you know that it is happening and that it is going to change. When you tell them, at the beginning of the course, that you're counting class participation in the grade, state that you're referring to the quality of the participation and that you don't welcome conversational monopolists. Maintain this policy throughout the course. It's easy to sit back and let one or two students take over, but it's harmful. Some students actually do have more interesting things to say about writing than others, of course, but do your best to ensure that all students feel comfortable contributing. (By all means lower grades for verbal bullies.) The more frequent the contributor, the more likely that he or she is repeating himself or herself and needs a break.

It's recommended that you establish, explicitly or implicitly, a policy of constructive speech: don't allow students to tear each other down or to make invidious personal comments under the cloak of "workshopping." And do remember that you are the authority in the classroom; your opinion, whether students believe it or not, counts more than theirs.

This leads to the second major hazard of a user-friendly classroom: the potential for deterioration of discipline. Your personal style and tone should maintain classroom order without being overbearing. That sounds like a difficult trick, but in fact it can come about almost magically if, from the beginning, you treat students with respect while making it clear that you expect them to adhere to certain standards and meet certain demands. You want them to have good discussions and you want them to write whatever their muses dictate, but you expect them to turn in such-and-such an amount of work at such-and-such intervals—and if they don't their grades will suffer accordingly, with the ultimate penalty, for the student who slacks off completely and makes no good-faith attempt to do the work, being failure in the course. Yes, creative writing is a fun course and grading is usually generous, but, no, they will not be allowed to duck your requirements.

If you can establish that kind of regimen—or some equally effective regimen in your own style—you'll run a good course.

# Chapter by Chapter: A Survey of the Book

## Chapter 1: Why We Write

### Chapter Summary

The book begins self-referentially, with a description of the author sitting down to write this book. It might be a portrait of any writer experiencing the anxiety of facing a blank page. Underlying the anxiety, however, is the confidence that the writer has gone through the experience before and knows how to deal with the emotions attendant upon success and failure. The confidence come from experience and discipline— the kind of discipline that *Writer's Mind* hopes to facilitate.

The process of facing a blank page every day is a kind of lifelong roller-coaster ride; why, then, do we willingly undergo it? The chapter examines some of the major motives for becoming a writer. For the money and fame? These are easily disposed of as inadequate motives; the money is meager compared to other professional fields (and much less secure), while fame is a dubious reward—and even the most successful writers are barely famous compared to movie stars or athletes.

Another often-cited motive, and partially valid, is self-expression; yet if self-expression were all, writing would be no more than therapy. (And the kind of self-expression writers indulge in can alienate the people on whom they base their characters.) A larger reason is needed. The writer wants to create something beautiful, an aesthetic object that will, to whatever small degree, counteract the ugliness of the world. Yet this motive too is only partial and excessively noble-sounding. Fundamentally, writers write because they feel compelled to do so as a way of announcing their existence. Writing is both a calling—in the sense of a vocation—and a call—in the sense of a bird's song.

### Approaching the Text

This chapter is an inspirational overture to the book and can be combined with Chapters 2 and 3 in a single reading assignment if your schedule is tight. If you have time to discuss Chapter 1 at length, it can provide a springboard to students' discussion of their own motives for writing (or for imagining themselves as future writers). Ask students how the description of a writer's experiences, at the beginning of the chapter, makes them feel. Does writing sound exciting? Daunting? A bit of both? Ask students how much creative writing they've done in the past, and whether they feel their motives were similar to the ones discussed in the chapter.

Emerging very strongly from the chapter's first sentence onward is the personal tone that marks the entire book. You might ask students to describe and critique the tone and to discuss whether or not they prefer it to a more impersonal, "textbooky" tone.

## Departing from the Text

Individual students may disagree with the author's analysis of the reasons for writing. Urge students to cite as many different motives for writing as they can. Some students may find the discussion of motives unnecessary—they simply want to start writing fiction. They should be encouraged!

## More Exercises

1.  Make a two-column list of reasons to be a writer and reasons not to be a writer. Read your list aloud, with one class member writing down a master list. Which column wins?

2.  Hold a class debate on the pros and cons of becoming a creative writer.

3.  Write a short story about someone who wants to be a writer. What happens to the character's hopes as time passes? Furthermore, is a character's desire to be a writer enough of a subject for a good story? (See Chapter 3, "What to Write About.") What can you add to the character and his or her situation that would make the subject more interesting?

4.  On a scale of one to ten, with one representing "virtually no commitment" and ten representing "total commitment," mark the degree of your commitment to becoming a creative writer. You need not show it to anyone. As time goes on, in this course and afterward, redo this exercise and see how your commitment evolves.

5.  A long-term exercise: read the biographies and autobiographies of writers and interviews with writers. What motives do they give for their calling?

## Troubleshooting

Many students will be more interested in money and fame than the book counsels them to be; that's perfectly okay, for it marks the difference between eager adolescence and jaded middle age. For young writers, the dream of money and fame may provide an incentive to work, even if the dreamed rewards don't arrive. Encourage students to discuss their preconceptions of the rewards and trials of a writer's profession: does the disparaging of money and fame disillusion them, and, if so, what is their response? If their response is, "I'm going to keep writing anyway," they're displaying writer's mind.

## Basic Students

Ask students why they elected this course. (The answer, "It sounded like an easy course," can be met with the response, "Okay, but what do you hope you might get out of the writing experience?" You might also point out that if students are as honest in their creative writing as in this answer, they'll probably produce work worth reading.) Review students' answers after several have been given, and ask students to compare the answers with the motives discussed in the chapter. Accept all sincere answers, and point out that one of the things students will gain from the course will be the opportunity to express themselves as they're presently doing.

## Advanced Students

Invite students to challenge the chapter: If they were writing the first chapter of a fiction-writing textbook, what would they say?

Invite students to discuss and analyze the style of the work. What do they like or dislike about it? What are the recognizable devices and "calling cards" of the author's style?

## For Discussion

- Does a writer need to understand why he or she writes before beginning to write? Why or why not?
- How might a writer's reasons for writing change during the course of a lifetime?
- Many people start out in life wishing they were writers; only a small percentage carry out that desire. Why?
- What's the most admirable motive for writing you can think of? What's the least admirable?
- How might a writer's motives for writing differ depending on the time, place, and culture the writer lives in?

# Chapter 2: What Is A Story?

## Chapter Summary

The basic unit of fiction is the story. (In this book's terms, *story* encompasses narratives of all lengths, including both the short story and the novel.) A story is defined as "the narrative of a sequence of significant events that happen to someone we care about." In this definition, the events and their significance, the characters and our concern for them, and the act of narration are all indispensable elements of storytelling. Sequence and specificity are also examined as essential elements of stories. It is proposed that storytelling is a basic, prehistoric, possibly preprogrammed form of human thought found in all cultures. A broader, more philosophical definition is then proposed: "A story is something we tell ourselves and temporarily believe." In this definition, most of human culture, including the development of ideologies and civilizations, can be seen as a form of storytelling.

## Approaching the Text

You might begin by asking, "Why do people tell stories?" or "Why do people like to listen to stories?" Narrow answers such as "to pass the time" or "because cave people didn't have television" might lead to broader exploration of the fact that storytelling is a universal human phenomenon. Storytelling isn't limited to literary fiction: we tell one another stories in explaining the world; we tell history in story form; we often think and dream in story form. Why do human beings spend so much of their time either producing or consuming this peculiar form of communication? The chapter alludes to these issues while setting out a definition of the literary story that is both practical and universal.

## Departing from the Text

For at least a hundred years, many fiction writers have expressed their irritation with the limits of the traditional story form (see Chapter 12, "Fancy Stuff"). Is it possible to write fiction without a story element? How far have experiments been taken in that direction? Young writers tend to be especially enthusiastic about nontraditional fiction and should be encouraged to try whatever new forms they can conceive of. (In most cases, this will boil down to imitating previous writers' experiments.) At the same time, the fact that people like stories is as inescapable as the fact that people are bipedal primates. The success of literary experiments may depend in part on finding workable substitutes for the gratifications of the traditional story.

## More Exercises

1.  What work of fiction that you know of is the least story-oriented? Bring it to class to read aloud (in whole or in part) and discuss.

2.  What is the best story you know, either in literature or in real life? Retell it orally. What makes it a great story?

3.  Read a folktale or fairy tale aloud to the class. After several students have done so, discuss what elements the stories have in common.

4.  Aside from "Once upon a time," what's the best way to begin a story? As a class, brainstorm a list of promising first lines.

## Troubleshooting

You may want to dissect the five-element definition of a story on page 9, examining each element to ascertain whether students agree that the element is fundamental.

The chapter's broad claims about the universality of narrative will interest philosophically-minded students; others will prefer to dwell on the practical elements of storytelling. The deliberately provocative statement, "There is no such thing as nonfiction" (page 12) is, of course, not intended literally. There is a type of writing we call nonfiction. We accept the proposition that nonfiction is about things that have happened, while fiction is about things that have not happened. But how do we determine what has happened? All human interpretations of experience are subjective. Any factual phenomenon may be described and narrated a hundred different ways by a hundred different eyewitnesses; the "facts" of the phenomenon are the interpretation reached by the consensus of observers.

## Basic Students

Have students, before the next class meeting, prepare a brief list of examples of story-telling they encounter in real life. This may include stories told among friends or family; explanations or excuses given to authorities; stories found in song lyrics, television shows, video games, and other entertainment; jokes and lies; news stories; dreams and daydreams; and other forms. Encourage students to find the five elements of the definition in the examples they give.

## Advanced Students

Some students may be interested in researching current literary, psychological, and anthropological theories on the function of narrative. Ask them to report briefly to the class.

## For Discussion

- Do you agree with the author's definition(s) of story? Propose an alternative of your own.
- Suppose the same events are narrated by several different storytellers. What is it about the individual storyteller's approach that makes each version different?
- What's the difference between a literary story and a myth?
- Think about the way you see the world, the way you think and feel. Is narrative an important part of your thought process, as the author claims? Elaborate.
- What does the author mean, "There is no such thing as nonfiction?"

# Chapter 3: What to Write About

## Chapter Summary

This chapter begins with a central paradox of writing: Depending on one's outlook, subject matter may make no difference or a great deal of difference. In theory, writers are free to choose whatever subject they like, and any subject can be the basis for a work of art; in practice, however, people tend to find some subjects more inherently dramatic than others, and the writer who chooses an inherently dramatic subject has an undeniable edge. The single, eternal subject of fiction is the passage of human beings through the stages of life. Specific subject categories in which these passages occur include: birth and childhood; growing up; love and its loss; marriage and the lack of it; family life and its conflicts; work; war; crime; illness and accident; the gain or loss of money; physical risk; death. Life's passages may also be explored in the context of institutions or time-limited processes: a journey or quest; a prison; a hospital; a job; a school; a military unit; a mission or case; an exploration or discovery; a career; and, most broadly, a life span. These institutions or processes are not exactly subjects but contexts in which subjects can be located.

## Approaching the Text

If you ask students, "What's the hardest part of writing for you?" most will answer, "Finding ideas to write about." This chapter is intended to help them in their search by pointing out the recurring processes of human life that have served as the basis for stories in all eras and cultures. The lists of subject categories, institutions, and processes may prove especially useful. Point out that most people experience most of these life-passages, but that each such experience is unique; in addition, any fictional character can be imagined to go through the same passages, equally uniquely. The infinite individuality of the ways in which they do so makes for a potentially infinite supply of subjects for fiction.

## Departing from the Text

Point out that the broad subject categories listed in the chapter are just starting points, too general to serve as story premises. "Love," "growing up," and so forth are not subjects but categories into which subjects can be classified. Thinking about the categories can help a writer find a subject. What turns the category into a subject is the individualization of the loving, the growing up, and so forth, of a specific character or characters (usually through setting, plot, and characterization). Ideally, a fictional subject doesn't duplicate any previous work but is representative of human experience.

## More Exercises

1. As a small group, arrive at a story subject by consensus; then let each member independently write his or her own story on that subject.
2. As a class, brainstorm a list of at least a dozen works of fiction students have read. Try to locate the works' subjects within the categories listed in this chapter. Do any lead you to new categories? Are any uncategorizable?
3. Try making a cluster diagram as a way of finding subject matter. Use any of the categories listed in this chapter as a key word or phrase; write it in the center of a sheet of paper. Free-associating, use the rest of the page to write down words and phrases that occur to you when thinking about the key term. Show the relationships among ideas by connecting the words and phrases with lines. As you write outward from the center, you're likely to arrive at more specific, concrete words and phrases. Steer your imagination toward inventing fictional situations and characters; for instance, if your key word is *love*, one entry in your cluster diagram might be "first love," which might lead you to a somewhat fictionalized entry, "two teenagers in the projects," and then to a more fully fictionalized entry, "they come from ethnic groups that are in conflict." Jotting spontaneously, you might fill in further details of plot, character, setting, and theme.

## Troubleshooting

Some students may feel that all subjects for fiction are equally valid and that only the writer's skill makes a difference. This is an honorable artistic position to take, one that this book does not disagree with. Discussion of the relative attractiveness of various subjects is a response to practical realities—readers like some subjects better than others—rather than a concern of pure art.

If students feel that the chapter's lists of subjects are incomplete or flawed, they should be encouraged to improve the lists.

If, after reading this chapter and trying its suggestions, students still feel at a loss for story subjects, they will probably appreciate your assigning one. Choose one from the "Do It" exercises for this chapter or another chapter. Alternatively, have students write a story using the subject matter of a story they have read for an English course but changing the plot, characters, and setting. Another alternative is to have students read today's newspaper, choose the story they feel contains the greatest human interest, and fictionalize it.

## Basic Students

Have students keep a log for about a week, listing the subject matter of every story they encounter in fiction or real life. Encourage them to locate those subjects within the chapter's categories.

Students who are entirely unable to come up with a subject for a story may be allowed to use the same subject as a classmate, as long as they write their own independent stories—and, of course, as long as the classmate agrees.

## Advanced Students

Have students, independently or in a group, read the latest issue of the *New York Times Book Review* and note the subject matter of every work of fiction reviewed, advertised, or briefly noted. What trends do students observe?

For historical comparison and contrast, have students do the same for issues of the *Times Book Review* from twenty-five years ago and from fifty years ago (available in microfilm at many libraries).

## For Discussion

- When you read fiction, how important do you feel the subject matter is to your enjoyment of the work?

- Think about the fiction you've read in the past couple of years. What subjects seem to be your favorites? How would you compare your tastes with those of the general public?

- F. Scott Fitzgerald once said that there are only two basic stories: "Cinderella" and "Jack the Giant-Killer." What did he mean? How valid do you think his insight was? If possible, add one or more primal stories to Fitzgerald's list.

- A nineteenth-century humorist, observing that stories about Lincoln, doctors, and dogs were all very popular at that time, suggested that the surest title for a bestseller would be *Lincoln's Doctor's Dog*. Brainstorm titles that would express today's most popular subjects.
- Why is it so hard to think of genuinely original subject matter?

## Chapter 4: Action Versus Plot

### Chapter Summary

People often think of action and plot as synonymous, but there is a crucial distinction between the two. Action consists of the events in a story: it is a quantitative thing. Plot is the way the events are organized into a logically connected, compelling whole: it is a structural thing. A successful plot may contain a lot of action or a little action; it may be "high-concept" or low-key. It should display continuity through the linkage of incidents by causation and motivation. Thus, plot and characterization are fundamentally joined, and the best way to think about one's plot is to think about one's characters—who are they, what is driving them, what will they do next?

### Approaching the Text

The great majority of students will have prior knowledge of plotting, through their experiences watching films and TV shows as well as reading and hearing stories. Involve this prior knowledge as a way of getting into the subject. Ask questions like, "What are some movies you've seen that struck you as having especially good plots? (Could you briefly summarize the main points of the plot for us?) What made those plots compelling? Have you seen movies or read stories where you thought the plot was well-constructed even though the action was low-key, without a lot of violence or melodramatic action? What made those plots work?

### Departing from the Text

Some students may wish for a more formulaic approach to plot—something that's easily provided. The basic steps in a traditional plot have been summarized as follows, with slight variations of wording, in numerous writers' manuals:

1.  A protagonist (with whom, ideally, the audience identifies or sympathizes) is faced, as soon as possible in the story, with an urgent conflict: something the protagonist must do or deal with or overcome but is prevented from immediately doing by external and/or internal obstacles.

2.  The protagonist's initial effort to solve the problem leads to a further development, or complication, of the problem; efforts to solve the first complication lead to a second complication, and so on, creating a causally and motivationally linked chain of complications.

3. Each complication increases dramatic tension, until a crisis point is reached, when the protagonist must either finally resolve the initial conflict or succumb.

4. By this point, the protagonist has gained enough experience to resolve the conflict in a way that brings either success or new insight (for the character and/or the reader) in defeat. (A successful resolution implies comedy; new insight in defeat implies tragedy.)

These steps can be summarized using four "c" words: conflict, complications, crisis, conclusion.

## More Exercises

1. Invent a plot involving an object—a school desk, a map, a sandwich, or anything else.

2. Open the dictionary at random and put your finger on any word. Invent a plot that takes off from that word. (Obviously, if you choose a word that seems to have no plot potential, randomly choose another.)

3. Invent a plot about an extraordinary surprise that might happen to you, or someone you know, tomorrow.

4. Invent the plot of an unhappy love story involving two people who seem to be ideally matched.

5. Invent the plot of a happy love story involving two people who seem to be badly matched.

6. Invent a plot in which the characters are not human.

7. Invent a plot about your favorite historical figure—something you're sure did not happen to that person in real life.

8. Write a short story that has the busiest plot you can invent.

9. Write a short story whose plot can be summarized in one sentence.

10. Write a short story in which there is only one event.

11. Write a one-paragraph summary of a plot that you think would be effective on the screen but not in print—or vice versa.

12. Write the story of your life in a page or so, changing whatever you need to in order for it to have a well-constructed plot.

## Troubleshooting

Some students, particularly the more literary-minded, may object to the idea that plotting is indispensable to fiction; they may prefer plotless fiction. Challenge them to cite works that are truly plotless. Most works that are conventionally plotless, such as the plays of Chekhov or Beckett, actually contain considerable narrative interest, but the conflicts are largely psychological, and the subjects and settings are taken from the lives (or fantasies) of ordinary people. There is still a "What's going to happen next?" interest. You might point out that such works are, in many cases, *more* skill-fully plotted than works that rely on obvious actions such as gunplay or car chases. Blatant, high-action devices are often a *substitute* for good plotting: they provide the audience with a jolt regardless of structural and characterological appropriateness.

## Basic Students

Ask students to write brief summaries of the most recent works of fiction or drama (including screen drama) they have read or seen. Invite them to discuss what aspects of these plots they considered well-done and what aspects they thought were weak or unsatisfying.

## Advanced Students

Study plotting in works of great literature your students are familiar with: the works of Shakespeare, Greek tragedy, the *Iliad* and *Odyssey*, or classic novels. How impor-tant is plotting in these works, and why? Can students imagine great works by the same authors, but lacking plot—what would they be like? In what ways do classic plots resemble the plots of modern entertainment? In what ways are they different?

   These questions may lead to more general ones such as: Why do people get hooked on plots? What are plots for? What do plots do?

   Similar questions are examined from a critical perspective in *Reading for the Plot: Design and Intention in Narrative*, Peter Brooks (Alfred A. Knopf, 1984).

## For Discussion

- Is there such a thing as a plot that has too much action? How so?
- Is a completely plotless story possible, or is there some minimal amount of narra-tive interest that must be present even in avant-garde experimental fiction?
- What are the best-plotted works of fiction you know? As a class, write a list so that students who have not already read those works can do so.
- Based on your experience as a reader and viewer, what single piece of advice would you give to a writer trying to create a good plot?

# Chapter 5: Characterization

## Chapter Summary

This chapter is the longest in Part One, because characterization is the hallmark of good fiction. If you have been devoting one week to each chapter, you might want to spend two weeks on this one, dividing it after the middle of page 51. Pages 35–51 set forth the eight basic ways in which characters are revealed to readers: through their names, their physical appearances, their personal histories, the things they say, the things others say about them, the ways they act in response to specific situations, the ways they act habitually, and their thoughts. The remainder of the chapter deals with the complexity and mutability of character: people don't always act in character, their personalities may or may not have stable cores, and our knowledge of others (and ourselves) is always incomplete. Composite characterization is recommended as a method of inventing new people. The chapter as a whole urges writers to make their characterizations as deep as possible, refuting the view that fictional characters must be simplified in order for readers to comprehend them.

## Approaching the Chapter

You might begin by asking students to name fictional characters who have stuck in their minds long after reading about them. Discuss what makes a good characterization: Vividness of outline? Psychological depth? Eccentric touches? The reader's sympathy? Perhaps all of these can be found in students' examples. You might then ask students to discuss how important they feel characterization is in fiction. Is it less important than plot, as important, more important? Does the answer depend on the kind of fiction? On the reader? On the writer's culture? There are no absolute answers, but the book presents answers—opinions—of its own. These abstract questions can lead to the pragmatic question, "How do writers create characters?" The eight basic techniques discussed in this chapter are the answer.

## Departing from the Text

The chapter presents a traditional vision of the well-rounded fictional character, augmented by the ideal of "striking through the mask"—piercing the outward facade of the social person and finding the more fluid, relatively chaotic, infinitely intricate self underneath. "Striking through the mask" is admittedly an ideal that even the greatest writers have trouble meeting; no student writer should be expected to fulfill it, but the presentation of an ideal is a valuable act in itself.

Some students may be more enthusiastic than others about the importance of characterization. Writers who consider themselves realists may be most enthusiastic, genre writers and experimentalists less so. In reality, different forms and genres of fiction do place varying emphases on characterization, and it is easy enough to cite famous works of fiction whose characterizations are two-or-one dimensional; nevertheless, three-dimensional characterization is a worthwhile goal for all writers.

## More Exercises

1.  Write a character sketch of someone who is the same sex as you, but whose personality is the opposite of yours.
2.  Write a character sketch of someone who is exactly like you except that only one important trait has been changed (other than sex).
3.  Write a character sketch of someone you would fall in love with—and make that person seem real, not ideal.

4.  Write a character sketch of someone from history or the media whom you admire, showing that person to be a complex, flawed individual.

5.  With one or more partners, brainstorm a list of as many personality traits as you can think of in five or ten minutes. Create composite characters by randomly choosing three or four traits for each.

6.  Choose someone you know very well. Describe that person without making any reference to his or her physical traits.

7.  Invent a new physical appearance for the person you described in exercise 6. Then, if you wish, change some aspects of the character's personality to fit his or her new appearance. Finally, invent a name for the character.

8.  Write a paragraph in which you describe the physical appearance of a fictional person you invent spontaneously. Then add a paragraph or more in which you describe a personality that might go with the appearance.

9.  Write a description of yourself the way someone who loves you sees you, then a description of yourself as seen by someone who doesn't love you.

10. Make a list of five ways of behaving that are habitual with you and one or more actions you've taken that go against the trend of your habits. (Alternatively, do this for a person you know or for a fictional character you've invented.)

11. Write a fictional biography, one-half to two pages long, of someone you know but whose real-life background you're not familiar with.

12. Select a favorite work of fiction. Invent a new character who might belong in the sequel.

## Troubleshooting

Some students may feel that a person's name and physical appearance have nothing to do with his or her personality. This is an admirable sentiment that may be true in some cases but in other cases is certainly not true. You might ask students to evaluate themselves and people they know in this light.

## Basic Students

A vivid outline characterization consisting of one or two memorable traits is a realizable goal. Home in on the eightfold list of characterization techniques. Of these, physical appearance (and, of course, naming a character) may be the easiest for students to accomplish. Describing one character by means of what another character says may be easier for many students than characterization through what the focal character himself or herself says or does: it's easier to have Jane say, "I think Joe's insecure," than to show Joe's insecurity through his words and actions. The technique should not be overdone—but you might point out that it's used a lot in soap operas.

## Advanced Students

Encourage students to analyze characterization in works of literature they study this year. How do the authors use the techniques discussed in this chapter? Do they use any other techniques, and, if so, what and how? Which characterizations are complex and which are simple? Encourage students to think of ways to improve the characterizations in the works they read.

You might suggest this exercise: Take a character you have previously written about, and write two versions of him or her. (They may be revisions of a previous story or new stories.) In one version, increase the number of traits the character displays and the number of other characters he or she interacts with; in the other version, decrease those two variables. Change any other aspects of the story that these character changes require. Which approach do you prefer and why?

## For Discussion

- The author's opinions aside, what do *you* think is the difference between a fictional character and a real person?
- In your opinion, which authors are most skillful at characterization and which are least skillful? Cite examples from their work.
- Are people always the same everywhere, or does human personality differ from era to era and culture to culture? Elaborate. If you believe there are "core" human traits or emotions—universals—list them.
- How might human personality change in the future?

# Chapter 6: Dialogue

## Chapter Summary

Dialogue is characterization; dialogue is information; dialogue is foreshadowing; dialogue is description; dialogue lets the writer test out ideas; dialogue does several things at once—it conveys characterization and plot and theme, cloaked in the colloquial, sometimes offhand, remarks of people talking to each other. Dialogue differs from conversation in that it contains much more meaning per line. Well-written dialogue sounds as if real people might speak it, but it has had all its fat stripped away. It is the opposite of idle chatter, though it may sometimes be disguised as idle chatter. (If long-windedness is an element of a character's identity, the trick is to convey the impression of long-windedness in a compressed form.)

## Approaching the Text

If your class is currently studying a work of fiction that contains an appreciable amount of dialogue, you might begin by having volunteers read aloud the dialogue of the characters, then having the class discuss the passages analytically. "What does this line of dialogue do?" is the overarching question that can be asked of any fictional speech. Encourage students to point out ways in which specific lines of dialogue work toward building characterization, plot, and theme. Also lead students to distinguish the individual speaking styles—or lack of them—in characters' dialogue. This kind of analysis can also be done for students' writing. Help students acquire the habit of searching for, and deleting or revising, nonfunctional dialogue. Passages of dialogue that make contributions to plot, character, and theme deserve commendation. Ideally, such contributions should be nonredundant: they should not merely duplicate the contributions made by previous passages but should present new insights or variations.

Reading plays is a good way to learn the functions of dialogue. Henrik Ibsen (*The Master Builder, An Enemy of the People, A Doll's House, Hedda Gabler*, etc.) is perhaps the supreme example of a playwright in whose work every line sounds natural, but every line performs at least one function in the architecture of the whole.

## Departing from the Text

Not all fiction needs dialogue. American readers are accustomed to seeing a certain percentage of dialogue on the typical page, but European fiction, particularly that of Germany and Central Europe, often presents a denser surface. The novels and stories of Franz Kafka are accessible works in which to analyze the effects of an absence of dialogue. You might ask students to imagine what stories such as "The Metamorphosis," "Investigations of a Dog," or "The Burrow" would be like if they contained the conventional percentage of dialogue: what might be gained, and what lost?

On the other hand, while this chapter argues for a compact style of dialogue, there's no denying that there are many works of published fiction in which the dialogue runs on at length, little different from chatty conversation. Whether this is a strength or a weakness is a question students might wish to discuss.

A British novelist whose grimly satirical novels consist almost entirely of dialogue is Ivy Compton-Burnett.

## More Exercises

1.  From memory, write down everything that has been said in class so far today. (This exercise can be done five or ten minutes after class has started.)

2.  Think of a commonplace expression people use all the time, such as "How are you?" or "Nice weather we're having." Write it down, and then write down as many ways as you can think of to say essentially the same thing in different words. For instance, "How are you?" can become, "Hello," "How ya doin'?" "Yo, what's happening?" "How lovely to see you again," and so forth. Once you've completed your list, invent a different character for each variation—a person who might believably use that speech style. Describe each character in a couple of sentences. (Taken further, students could then describe possible inter-

actions among two or three of their characters and then write short stories based on this planning: a case of making something out of nothing!)

3.   Write a short story that consists almost entirely of dialogue. The dialogue should be functional—it should contribute to plot, character, and meaning.

4.   Rewrite one of your short stories as a short play.

5.   Choose a published short story that contains little or no dialogue. (The stories of Hawthorne and Poe make good candidates.) Rewrite it either as a short play, or as a short story containing significantly more dialogue.

6.   Write a philosophical dialogue, à la those of Plato, on an abstract question or idea that interests you, giving each character a distinct intellectual position.

7.   Write down the conversations that have been going on in your head during the past five or ten minutes.

8.   Write a dialogue between a character from your culture and a character from another culture. (Define "culture" any way you feel is appropriate.) Make the speech of both characters true to life and not stereotypical.

## Troubleshooting

Dialogue tends to be a strength of student writers, and this strength should be positively reinforced. The danger is that student stories can be chat-heavy. It may be asking too much, however, for students to correct this problem, since their dialogue is so often realistic and engaging. It's certainly a preferable problem to student stories that bog down in pseudo-lyrical description. Only a truly gifted student writer can reach the point of deleting clever lines in order to distill dialogue.

Students who seem to have a tin ear for dialogue can practice making transcriptions of actual conversations they hear, even very brief ones. They can analyze such transcriptions to find individual speech styles. The next step is to use their imaginations to fill in the forgotten portions of conversations that they partly remember. The next step is to invent entire conversations. The key, always, is to link dialogue to character: urge students to keep a picture of the speaking character in mind and to hear the character's voice speaking the lines.

Rereading one's dialogue aloud is a time-honored method of testing it during the revision stage.

## Basic Students

For students who have trouble getting anything at all on paper, dialogue is a good way of loosening up, since, at the beginning at least, they can transcribe real conversations, exerting no pressure on their imaginations.

To learn about individual speech styles, students can work with partners. A pair might talk for two or three minutes about any subject that interests them; then, working together, they can write down what they remember saying. They can then look for differences in their speech styles.

Students who like to watch television can be urged to listen for, and write examples of, the speech styles of their favorite characters or celebrities. Once a student has studied the speech style of a television personality, he or she can then make up new dialogue for that personality.

## Advanced Students

Challenge students to write dialogue for characters from literature.

Urge students to improve their dialogue by eliminating all nonfunctional speeches and by making sure that each character has a distinct speech style.

Some students may be interested in analyzing changes in the style of literary dialogue during the history of modern Western fiction—say, from the eighteenth century to today.

## For Discussion

- When you read fiction, do you usually like reading the dialogue, or do you find it tedious and sometimes skip over it? Explain your preference.
- Imagine a book the length of a novel, consisting entirely of transcribed real-life conversation. What would be its strengths and weaknesses?
- Do you think writers should use nonstandard spelling and punctuation for characters from other cultures? How about nonstandard vocabulary and grammar? Give reasons.
- Are there functions in fiction that dialogue *can't* perform or can't perform well? If so, what are they?

# Chapter 7: How to Describe Things

## Chapter Summary

There are as many different ways of writing descriptions as there are individual writers, but this chapter recommends a basic, overall approach that's adaptable to many individual styles. Simplicity is its principle. Student writers should not be encouraged to strain to find fancy words in a misguided attempt at sounding literary; plain words often make the most vivid descriptions. A principle of fact-reporting is proposed: each descriptive sentence or clause should present the reader with new information, rather than simply repeating previous details in different words. Another useful principle is that of image separation: sensory imagery tends to be more distinct when each object is assigned to a grammatical unit that can stand on its own—a sentence or an independent clause. (For this reason, simple or compound sentences often make for more vivid description than complex sentences containing subordinate clauses.)

## Approaching the Text

Ask students to read aloud paragraphs of description from a variety of sources that they think are excellent. Possible sources include published fiction, student fiction, and published nonfiction. Point out that there are many ways of describing things, from the very simple to the very ornate, but that this chapter presents sensible broad principles that can contribute to any writer's descriptive approach. The simplicity, fact-reporting, and image separation that are recommended here can be viewed as "default" positions—good to use in the absence of a specific preference for using another way. The author personally admires ornate, even torrential, description, several examples of which are included in this chapter's "Writer's Bookshelf," but simple description is a much more universally applicable, practical foundation for both the apprentice and the professional.

## Departing from the Text

As the above comments imply, student may be given plenty of latitude in departing from the philosophy of simple, fact-based description and should be encouraged to experiment with whatever descriptive styles appeal to them. Only a writer with a special verbal talent is likely to find a more effective personal descriptive style, however. Such writers are not likely to be hurt by the discipline of temporarily moderating their extravagances, while the writer of average or even above-average lyrical gifts will gain by striving for simplicity.

## More Exercises

1. Describe your own face, with or without looking in a mirror.
2. Describe an emotion without naming it. Do so by describing an object, place, or event through the eyes of someone feeling the emotion.
3. Describe a specific place or building that you are familiar with, using as few adjectives and adverbs as possible.
4. Imitating the style of your favorite writer, describe a landscape.
5. Describe today's weather in more than two hundred words; then in fewer than twenty words. (Make the short description vivid and original; don't settle for a cliché like, "It's a bright sunny day.")
6. Describe another planet, either real or imaginary, from any viewpoint you choose.
7. Assume you are an extraterrestrial who has secretly visited Earth. Write a brief report describing one significant feature of this planet or its life.
8. Describe what it's like to be born.
9. Describe what it's like to die or to witness death.
10. Describe something you have never read a description of before.

## Troubleshooting

As readers, many students don't like description. If you ask, "When you read a story, what passages are you most likely to skip over?" the answer is almost invariably, "The descriptions." This is precisely why it's important for writers to learn to write better descriptions—so that readers don't skip over them! And simplicity—conciseness—is one way to achieve that. Another crucial point of understanding, discussed in the chapter, is that good descriptions do more than physically create scenes: they can enhance characterization, tone, mood, and theme. The more such functions a descriptive passage performs, the less likely a reader is to skip it.

## Basic Students

Basic students may have a tendency to underdescribe: to have difficulty reaching for the vivid nouns and verbs, the "exact and happy" (in John Updike's phrase) modifiers that, no matter how concise, make a strong sensory image. Encourage them to try to visualize details before writing them down. Doing pencil sketches will help some students visualize what they're going to write about. Reassure them that they needn't use a complex vocabulary in describing things, nor need they write long, thick descriptions. They must, however, choose precise, concrete words.

## Advanced Students

In contrast to basic students, advanced students sometimes have a tendency to overdescribe as a way of showing off their vocabularies. This is exacerbated by the fact that the standard textbook approach to description encourages purple prose, through such misguided advice as "Use vivid, descriptive adjectives and adverbs." Students should be reminded that there's no such thing as a "descriptive" word in contrast to other kinds of English words; a descriptive word is an ordinary word that happens to be used to describe something. Discourage students from using a "literary" palette—from writing *luminous* instead of *glowing*, *mire* instead of *mud*, *verdant* instead of *green*, *cascaded* instead of *fell*. That's stale, corny, and old-fashioned, though there are still writers who write that way. Convey Mark Twain's advice: "As to the adjective—when in doubt, strike it out."

Encourage students to find examples of purple prose in published writing and to revise such passages.

Invite students to write descriptive passages that parody their favorite (or least favorite) writers.

## For Discussion

- Since we have photographs and movies, what's the point of using words to describe things?
- Which writers you are familiar with are the most skilled at description?
- What aspects of descriptive writing do you like and what aspects annoy you? Provide examples.

- In your opinion, how much description is enough in the typical fictional scene?
- What can description do aside from physically describing things?

## Chapter 8: Narration and Dramatization

### Chapter Summary

A fictional scene can be rendered in two basic ways: It can be narrated or dramatized. Narration compresses a scene into a summary of events; dramatization elaborates upon selected details fully enough for the reader to imagine sensory data and the passage of time. In most fiction, there is an alternation of narrated and dramatized passages, depending on the writer's sense of pacing and of the relative importance of events. The famous (or infamous) dictum, "Show, don't tell," urges the writer to illustrate a scene with sensory data rather than summarizing or explaining it with facts; yet it's not true that every scene should be dramatized and that nothing should ever be narrated in summary fashion. The chapter examines the meanings of this dictum and discusses its usefulness and limitations. Above all, "Show, don't tell" should not become a prescription for purple prose or for the abandonment of straightforwardness.

The chapter ends with a discussion of transitions and a recommendation that they be used economically.

### Approaching the Text

You might begin by selecting two passages, one of them narrated and the other dramatized, from a work of fiction your class has been studying. Read them aloud, and ask students to discuss the differences in their approaches to scene-rendering. Then introduce the terms *narration* and *dramatization*, and point out which is which.

### Departing from the Text

Students are likely to have come across the dictum, "Show, don't tell," in previous English classes and may very well have been puzzled about its meaning, for what was once a piece of revelatory off-the-cuff editorial advice has since been inappropriately carved in stone. The chapter provides synonyms: "Illustrate, don't explain," and "Be concrete, not abstract." The chapter also presents a critique of a widespread abuse of the dictum. Examples of "showing, not telling" in standard textbooks often leave the impression that pulpy, turgid descriptions are preferable to brisk, straightforward ones; students may have come away from previous courses fearing that they're never allowed to state anything directly. The discussion in this chapter is intended to correct that. Used correctly, "Show, don't tell" means, "Bring scenes to life; don't leave them flat."

A similar critique is presented for the overuse of transitional words and phrases in prose. Transitions are more important in expository and persuasive writing than in creative writing, and even in those areas, the author feels that transitions have been overemphasized in recent years. Excessive use of transitions slows prose down and goes against the grain of contemporary media such as music videos and TV commercials, in which transitions are truncated or absent. You may wish to present the minimizing of transitions in fiction writing as an exception to an overall recommendation in favor of transitions.

You might discuss this critique, comparing and contrasting it to other approaches students have been exposed to, as an exercise in critical thinking.

## More Exercises

1.  Recall a story you've read or written recently. From memory, write a narrative summary of it in one paragraph.
2.  Find one example of narration and one example of dramatization in any published work of fiction. Rewrite them, expanding the narrated scene into a dramatized one and compressing the dramatized scene into narrative.
3.  Select a short story you especially like. Write down, underline, or highlight every example of a transitional word or phrase in it. Discuss your observations and conclusions with classmates who have done the same.
4.  Find a successful example of "telling, now showing" in a published work of fiction you like.

## Troubleshooting

If students are still confused about narration versus dramatization and showing versus telling, try to get them to find examples of these approaches in fiction they have read or written. Discuss the relative effectiveness of the selected passages, and allow students to draw their own conclusions.

## Basic Students

The difference between narration and dramatization can be paraphrased as the difference between a quick, factual summary and a longer scene that includes lots of sensory detail. Encourage students to find examples of each in the fiction your class is reading this year. Reassure students that they don't have to get bogged down in the subtleties of understanding "Show, don't tell." What they—and more advanced students as well—really need is to develop a gut feeling for when to dilate a scene and when to compress it.

## Advanced Students

Ask students to compare the proportions of narration versus dramatization in fiction and folktales from various cultures and eras. On the whole, contemporary American fiction is well toward the "dramatization" end of the spectrum. Discuss what this implies: is dramatization more sophisticated than narration, or, on the other hand, could contemporary fiction gain vigor from a return to narration?

## For Discussion

- Why do narration and dramatization usually alternate in a work of fiction? Why not just pick one and stick with it?
- Which do you generally prefer reading (and writing), passages of narration or ones of dramatization? Why?
- What do you usually find easy, and what do you usually find hard, about writing narration and about writing dramatization?

# Chapter 9: Point of View and Narrative Distance

## Chapter Summary

Choosing a point of view is a crucial but relatively simple technical decision that affects the complexion of an entire work of fiction. The chapter defines and elaborates upon the major points of view: first person, omniscient third person, limited third person, and second person. The potential overlapping of the two forms of third person, and the possibility of variations within them, is emphasized. The second person is differentiated into second person declarative and second person imperative. The omniscient first-person is discussed as well. Strengths and weaknesses of each point of view are brought forward, along with tips on choosing a point of view.

Narrative distance (sometimes called psychic distance) is a related concept that operates in the microlevel of individual sentences, rather than the macrolevel of an entire work or scene. Having chosen a dominant point of view—for instance, first person—the writer can manipulate descriptions as if changing the angle of a movie camera shot, bringing the lens closer to the point of view character or drawing it farther away.

## Approaching the Text

Depending on your grade level, some or all students are likely to have encountered point of view in previous English courses. You might begin, then, by asking volunteers to define the concept and the major points of view. Then point out the overriding message of this chapter: that although point of view is a primary technical consideration, it isn't as mysterious or forbidding as it's sometimes made out to be; it can be reduced to a simple either-or decision: first person or third—a decision that's hard to make incorrectly.

If your students are completely unfamiliar with point of view, introduce the concept by reading differently viewpointed passages aloud from works of fiction they are familiar with. A chalkboard chart of the major viewpoints would be appropriate.

## Departing from the Text

Narrative distance is a more sophisticated concept than point of view; if you're teaching high school you'll want to concentrate on the latter, while if you're teaching college you may want to highlight the former as the aspect that's newer to students. For the average high school class, a nod of acknowledgment in the direction of narrative distance, with a recommendation that interested students ponder it on their own, is enough.

## More Exercises

1.  Write a story using the omniscient third-person point of view without entering the thoughts of any character.
2.  Rewrite the story you wrote for exercise 1, this time entering the thoughts of the protagonist.
3.  Rewrite the same story again, this time entering the thoughts of the protagonist and one or more other characters.
4.  Write a story in the first person in which the narrator is partly or wholly untrustworthy.
5.  Write a story in the first person in which the narrator is trustworthy as far as reporting events but unsympathetic in his or her personality.
6.  Write a story using the first-person plural point of view: the narrator is "we."
7.  Write a story in the first person, placing the narrative distance far from the narrator. Then rewrite it, bringing the narrative distance noticeably closer to the narrator.
8.  Reread a favorite story, paying close attention to the manipulation of narrative distance. Then write an imitation of the author's technique.

## Troubleshooting

All students should be able to distinguish the major points of view after brief instruction. If some students have trouble differentiating narrative distances, you may present it as a secondary concept that needn't be studied in detail (although from the perspective of the working writer, it's certainly important).

Some students may be surprised by the news that the choice of point of view can be an easy decision. After that initial reaction, the news will probably be welcome to them. Point of view is an area of technique in which writers too often let themselves bog down; this chapter tries to free their inhibitions about the choice.

## Basic Students

Have students identify the major points of view in passages from works of fiction the class is studying—either ones you have chosen or ones students locate on their own.

For purposes of their own writing, point of view should be made a simple binary choice: first person or third person. Once the choice is made, the important thing is to maintain consistency.

## Advanced Students

Shifting point of view within a short story was once considered taboo and is still quite difficult to accomplish successfully. For a short story in which the third person narrative enters the mind of several characters in succession (including a lion), recommend Hemingway's "The Short Happy Life of Francis Macomber."

Advanced students may be intrigued by the concept of narrative distance and may wish to study it in works of published fiction. Joyce and Woolf are two writers who handle this technique with supreme skill.

Encourage experiments with point of view! Refrain from adverse comments on the gimmicky, tricky viewpoints your students may want to play around with.

## For Discussion

- What difference does point of view make, anyway?
- The author presents point of view as a relatively simple, though important, technical decision. Do you share that assessment, or is choosing a point of view hard for you? Explain.
- What's the most interesting, original use of point of view you know of?
- What point of view do you feel most comfortable using, and why? Are there ones you don't feel comfortable with?
- How do you think your writing would be affected if you tried a point of view you didn't usually use? (Try it and see!)
- Do you have a favorite narrative distance as a writer and as a reader? What, and why?

# Chapter 10: Style, Voice, Tone

## Chapter Summary

This chapter covers three intertwining concepts that involve the way a writer uses words. Style is the broadest of the three and might be defined as the sum of all the distinctive, individualistic ways a writer uses words. (More broadly still, an era, a nation, or a culture can have a style.) Voice, a catchphrase of recent years, is the aspect of style that makes the words sound as if they were spoken by a human being. We can speak of a writer's voice—in which case the term really does not differ in meaning from "style"—but we can also talk about a writer's deliberately taking on one voice or another for a specific work or part of a work or of a writer's giving a distinctive voice to a specific character or narrator. Voice, in this sense, is a subset of style. Tone is a vocal quality of writing, which lends a specific feeling or attitude to the words—for instance, a gloomy tone, a satirical tone, an ironic tone, a cheerful tone.

## Approaching the Text

The chapter's opening paragraph, deliberately written in a pastiche of an antique style, is meant to initiate discussion as to what style means: is it a natural expression of personality, or can it be artificially adopted? Does a writer have one style or many? You might begin, even before discussing the chapter, by asking broad questions along these lines. Broadest of all would be, "What is style?" Suitable follow-up questions might include, "What do you think of when a teacher says that a particular writer has an interesting style?" "How important to you is the writer's style when you read fiction?" "Where does style come from?"

## Departing from the Text

Depending on their relative appeal to you, you might want to devote varying proportions of time and attention to the three concepts of style, voice, and tone. Style, as the broadest of the concepts, is perhaps the most nebulous, and in practice a style takes years to develop; students should not be expected to have a fully accomplished style within the scope of a course, but they can be guided toward sources of style—i.e., toward good literature. Voice has been a fashionable concept in recent years, and for that very reason deserves to be critiqued, yet it's true that much good writing (including this book!) conveys the quality of human speech. Perhaps the most direct single piece of practical advice that can be given to writers trying to achieve "voice" is, "Loosen up!" Encourage students to write colloquially, casting aside their preconceptions about what literature sounds like, and to avoid stuffiness and pretentiousness— unless, of course, they deliberately want to write in the voice of a stuffy, pretentious character.

One of the best ways to study style, voice, and tone is to read aloud (or have students read) from works that strongly display these qualities. Personal essays tend to have attractive, skillfully controlled voices.

## More Exercises

1. Write a passage of dialogue (approximately one page) between two siblings, one of whom is relaxed and easygoing, the other of whom is tense and suspicious. The topic is up to you. Make the nervous, suspicious sibling the narrator. Then write another draft in which the relaxed, easygoing sibling is the narrator.

2. Write a page in the first-person voice of a computer, on the topic, "My Life." After rereading it, think about what other styles, voices, tones, you might have used.

3. Write a character sketch of someone you know, in an ironic tone, in the third person.

4. Choose an object, place, or activity you like very much. Describe it in a negative tone—sad, gloomy, tragic.

5. Do the reverse of exercise 4: choose something you dislike very much and describe it in a happy, cheerful, comic tone.

## Troubleshooting

Tone is a concept many high school students find difficult to grasp. The key is to get students to realize that they employ and interpret a variety of tones all the time in their everyday conversation. So you might begin by proposing a topic (such as "school") and asking students to ad lib oral comments about it in a variety of tones. Or, ask students to recall examples of comments they've heard recently in a variety of tones—perhaps comments you and others have made in class. Once they've recognized their own prior knowledge of tone, they'll be better prepared to recognize it in writing. *Creating* a specific tone in writing is harder still, partly because tone depends on the hearer and the context: what's intended as humorous in tone may fall flat, what's intended as solemn may be unintentionally funny, and what's intended as ironic may be ham-handed. In general, students are safest when reproducing tones that match the ones they use in everyday life, rather than "literary" tones.

All student styles are derivative of other writers; this is not a problem at the apprentice stage, although it must be overcome if a writer is to pass beyond apprenticeship. It's common, and well-advised, for students to pass through a number of imitative phases in succession: Hemingway one month, Nabokov the next, and so forth, with each new influence helping counteract the previous ones and each leaving a residue within the student's developing personality. A frequent problem with students' derivative styles is that they tend to be either overwritten or underwritten, depending on the writer the student is (consciously or unconsciously) imitating. The student imitating hard-boiled fiction is apt to be so tight-lipped that his or her fiction leaves no room for the play of emotion or for three-dimensional description and characterization. The student imitating twentieth-century modernist styles is liable to develop logorrhea, displaying his or her vocabulary (and stamina) at the expense of wearing the reader out. Your role as instructor may be to simply, and gently, point out such problems, conveying to the student your confidence that it's all part of the learning process.

## Basic Students

If students have trouble identifying style, voice, and tone in literary works, they may be able to do so in comic books, which distinctly possess those traits.

If there's a skilled impressionist in your class, he or she may be able to mimic the tones of voice of various celebrities.

Literary style may be difficult for basic students to recognize and create. They may be more quick to recognize style in other spheres of life, however. Everyone has a personal style of dress, of behavior, of playing a given sport, of singing, of going to sleep at night and waking up in the morning, of doing homework—everyone has a personal style of doing everything. This is one of the wonders of existence: we're all made of the same chemical elements and the same kinds of genetic material, but we're all unique. Encourage students to cite aspects of their personal styles, or, if they prefer, to write thumbnail descriptions of their styles at doing the above-mentioned activities.

Encourage basic students to be natural in their writing styles but to use standard grammar and mechanics unless nonstandard is specially called for by the demands of characterization.

## Advanced Students

Advanced students may be interested in fooling around with a wide variety of styles—imitating published writers, imitating each other, imitating themselves, imitating other media (comics, movies, TV, etc.) in the form of print. The imitations may be parodistic or serious. Few students will want to stick with a style that's primarily parodistic, but all will gain from brief excursions.

## For Discussion

- An old adage says, "The style is the man." What does it mean? Do you agree or disagree, and why?
- If a style is the natural outgrowth of a personality, why do writers have to work at their styles? Or do they?
- Whose styles, among famous writers, do you like most? Dislike most?
- Is style more important in certain kinds of fiction than in others, and, if so, which ones?

# Chapter 11: Theme

## Chapter Summary

The chapter begins on a comical note, poking fun at scholarly criticism. The underlying serious point is that working writers usually analyze fiction (their own or others') differently from the way critics do. Most literary criticism in America today is interpretive: it seeks to find themes, symbols, ideological positions, or cultural biases in the work of fiction; it decodes the text with an eye toward reading a hidden or partially hidden meaning. Students are likely to have absorbed this approach in their literature studies, and it's a valid approach from the critic's or reader's standpoint. The fiction writer, however, approaches a work of fiction as a construction: something to be built as solidly as possible by means of certain techniques and effects. The writer may have themes in mind, but in building the work, he or she treats the themes as functional elements of plot, characterization, and style. If concern for sending a message outweighs concern for aesthetics, the work becomes propaganda, and probably boring. If theme is treated as an element of aesthetics, it emerges organically, with its complexities and ambiguities intact, from the personalities and behaviors of the characters.

Part of the training for becoming a writer, therefore, involves learning how to read fiction from the writerly perspective rather than (or in addition to) the critical perspective. The student trained in interpretive criticism is likely to ask, "What does the work mean?" Reading as a creative writer, however, the student should get into the habit of asking questions such as, "How did the author achieve that effect? Why is this scene fully dramatized while that one is narrated? What future scene is this scene preparing for? How might that description have been improved? Does this scene work or doesn't it, and why?"

## Approaching the Text

You might begin by asking, "How important do you think theme is to writers when they write stories?" or perhaps, "When you write a story, how important is theme to you?" Point out that different writers have different views on this subject. Some, like Upton Sinclair or Alexander Solzhenitsyn, might feel that their message is foremost and that their duty is to shape the work in whatever way will most powerfully express that message; others, like Oscar Wilde, might only be concerned with the beauty and perfection of their work of art and not with its meaning. (Wilde once said, "Views are held by those who are not artists." Of course, that is a view.) Most writers probably fall between the two extremes. Being intelligent, literate people, they are aware of at least some of the possible interpretations of their work (not necessarily all the interpretations), and being citizens, they have opinions they might welcome the opportunity to express. Nevertheless, their primary duty is to write a successfully crafted work of art, and they know they're more likely to do so if they view their characters as complex human beings rather than as mouthpieces for ideas. A writer may privately hold strong views on an issue, but in fiction may deliberately explore competing sides of the issue in order to enhance the impression of lifelike ambiguity. A writer may write a story in which justice prevails, while privately suspecting that, in real life, justice does not prevail. And very often a writer observes the development of his or her own characters and plot in order to find out what his or her view of life is in the first place.

In short, a well-crafted work of fiction can be produced by a writer who is very much aware of its themes, by one who is completely indifferent to theme, or by any kind of writer in between.

## Departing from the Text

This chapter introduces a way of reading fiction that supplements the theme-oriented way students are used to. Students who prefer to read for theme rather than for craft are certainly entitled to keep that preference; as a matter of practical reality, it's more likely that a given student in a creative writing class will become a literature teacher, or a general reader, than that he or she will become a professional fiction writer. Even the future critic, however—perhaps especially the future critic—can benefit from learning a new way of reading. America's foremost poetry critic, Helen Vendler, states this craft-oriented approach in the introduction to her book *The Music of What Happens:* "Art must say something and must care about what it says; and every artist uses 'ideas' (as well as images, phonemes, echoes, textural contrast, feelings, myths, and so on) as part of the raw material of composition. The artist uses ideas, that is, as functional parts (rather than as ideological determinants) of the work."

## More Exercises

1.  Think of a theme or thesis that appeals to you and that can be stated in one or two sentences. It may concern public life (e.g., "Ideology often serves as a smokescreen for ethnic cruelty") or private life (e.g., "True love is only possible between equals"). Write a story in which your main conscious purpose is to illustrate that theme. Compare and contrast this writing experience, and its results, with your usual work.

2.  Choose a short story that you have read recently and liked. On a sheet of paper divided into two columns, make notes for two different analyses of the work: on the left side from the standpoint of a literary critic concerned with the work's meaning; on the right side from the standpoint of a writer concerned with the work's craft.

3.  Write a response to the ideas expressed in this chapter, based on your own experiences as a writer.

## Troubleshooting

As was implied in "Approaching the Text" and "Departing from the Text," students are likely to hold a variety of opinions on the importance of theme to the creative writer. Accept all such opinions and present them together (perhaps in a list) as a repertoire of viewpoints that can all be useful for writers. This chapter presents one such position but, as always, encourages each writer to form his or her own philosophy. After all, if ideas are simply tools for building art, then any critical approach can serve as such a tool.

The most liberating implication in this chapter, perhaps, is that a work of fiction does not have to have a thesis. The writer of a story about family life is not obliged to come down on the side of either approving or disapproving of the family as an institution. If the writer *creates* a family, that's enough; readers can do the interpreting.

## Basic Students

Basic students are likely to need practice in reading from both the meaning-oriented critical perspective and the craft-oriented writerly perspective, and the former is the one they'll encounter more often in their school careers. Emphasize that when a writer pays attention to craft, it strengthens a work's meaning—the two approaches are not mutually exclusive. The best way to make this point is to analyze a great work of literature students are familiar with (perhaps a poem) and discover how style and technique reinforce theme.

## Advanced Students

You might read students the Vendler quote, above, as a springboard for discussion on the nature of literary criticism. Add that Vendler divides criticism into three camps: *interpretive* (finding meaning in a work), *ideological* (uncovering the author's or the culture's values), and *aesthetic* (studying a work as a constructed object whose aim is beauty).

## For Discussion

- Which interests you more when you read fiction, the meaning of a work or its craftsmanship? How about when you write fiction? (There's no need to think the correct answer is "craftsmanship" just because you're in a creative writing class!)
- Of the fiction writers you're familiar with, which ones do you think paid most attention to theme? Least? (Look for interviews with these writers, if possible, to help answer this question.)
- The chapter puts forward different ideas about the role of theme in fiction. Do these ideas necessarily contradict each other or can they be reconciled? If they can be reconciled, how?

# Chapter 12: Fancy Stuff

## Chapter Summary

This chapter examines a number of fictional techniques that were considered experimental in the first half of the twentieth century but have since become part of the standard literary tool kit. Modernist writers have enlarged the range of what is possible in fiction, notably by shifting points of view, jumbling chronology, writing stream of consciousness, and incorporating elements of other literary forms (often parodistically) into fiction. The chapter points out that characterization may be the element of fiction that has been least affected by experimentalism, doubtless because it is harder to deepen one's understanding of human beings than to invent a technical or stylistic gimmick. The chapter ends in a call for action on this front—an admittedly utopian aim that no student should be expected to achieve.

## Approaching the Text

Elicit prior knowledge by asking students what have been the most difficult, most original, most experimental works of fiction they've encountered. In each case, ask the student to describe the innovations in the work. Inform students that this chapter provides a convenient summary of a number of innovations that have come about in the past century and even suggests a path toward future innovations.

## Departing from the Text

This chapter presents experimental fiction as an alternative to traditional craftsmanship, but for some students and writers it's more than that: it's their passion. Use such students as resources who can seek out, and keep the class informed about, vanguard fiction. At the same time, try to persuade them that traditional craftsmanship will not hurt them and is not limited to the domain of the stodgy; many experimentalist works use vestiges of story and character as a kind of ballast to anchor them in human experience and readability.

## More Exercises

1.  Discover a work of experimental fiction written in the past generation or so, one you haven't read before. (Do so by browsing at the library or bookstore, consulting a librarian, consulting a literature teacher, or reading literary criticism and book reviews.) Report on it to the class as part of an ongoing project in which the class will keep a file of interesting literary innovations.

2.  Imagine that you have been raised in a world without fiction—you have never read a story or novel before. Suddenly, out of the blue, you are inspired to write about human experience by making things up. You don't quite understand what such a work would be; you don't even have the name "fiction" for it. Lacking any models of previously written fiction, what will you write? Write it now—or write a description of what it would be like. (The description will be a work of fiction in itself.)

## Troubleshooting

Whether or not students use any of the modernist techniques described in this chapter should be left up to them, with this exception: you might find it worthwhile, once in each course—and only if you have time—to ask students to write a story using the modernist technique of their choice. This will give students a modicum of exposure to the techniques. After that, they can either explore this realm further or drop it.

## Basic Students

One might assume that basic students will be incapable of understanding innovative fiction, but that isn't necessarily the case. It depends on the individual work and its form. Certain media that are very popular with young people are experimentalist in their stance: music videos, MTV promos, animations, interactive fiction, and graphic (i.e., comic book) novels. You might be surprised to find out how knowledgeable your seemingly nonintellectual students are within these media. Ask *them* to teach *you* about them. Connect the techniques of those media with possible literary uses. A warning, however: works in these media, especially graphic novels, can be quite explicit in their use of sex and violence and dubious in their values. Never recommend a work you have not personally examined!

Commercial and independent movies, through their use of fragmented chronology and quick cutting, can also provide inspiration for literary experiments.

## Advanced Students

Even in advanced high school classes and many college classes, you may wish to steer students toward those modernist works that are comparatively readable.

Faulkner's *As I Lay Dying* is written, for the most part, in simple prose. Stein's *Three Lives* and *The Autobiography of Alice B. Toklas* are the most accessible of her works, though not the most innovative. Toni Morrison's *Jazz* and *Beloved* use modernist techniques to examine the African American experience, as do Charles Johnson's *Oxherding Tale* and *Middle Passage* (and Stein's "Melanctha" in *Three Lives*, for that matter). Marguerite Duras' *The Lover* is not only concise, but exists in a movie version *and* in a later novel version, *The North China Lover*, which Duras wrote in light of the movie. Günter Grass' *The Tin Drum* and Gabriel García Márquez's *One Hundred Years of Solitude* are essential texts of magic realism. Manuel Puig's *Betrayed by Rita Hayworth* is a novel of adolescence that uses Faulkneresque alternating narrators; Puig's *Heartbreak Tango* is a provincial romance that parodies radio soap operas. Jayne Anne Phillips' short story collection, *Black Tickets*, exemplifies a punk sensibility many students will like. Nicholson Baker's *Mezzanine* is a low-calorie, playfully literary novel that takes place almost entirely during an escalator ride. Science fiction writers J. G. Ballard, Thomas M. Disch, Joanna Russ, Samuel R. Delany, Stanislaw Lem, Sue Thomas, Harlan Ellison, William Gibson, and Jack Womack have rubbed up against literary experimentalism (Disch's great story "Descending" anticipated *Mezzanine*). In turn, mainstream writer Doris Lessing has written experimental science fiction in her *Canopus in Argos* series, as did Italo Calvino in *Cosmicomics*, while Anthony Burgess' *A Clockwork Orange* and Russell Hoban's *Riddley Walker* present youth-oriented, frightening visions of the future, in the voices of teenage narrators who speak invented jargons. Gore Vidal's *Duluth* uses Nabokovian techniques to present a comic vision of an alternative America. Umberto Eco's *The Name of the Rose*, Julian Barnes' *Flaubert's Parrot*, A. S. Byatt's *Possession*, and Jeanette Winterson's *Oranges Are Not the Only Fruit* are contemporary bestsellers with postmodern attitudes.

## For Discussion

- Why isn't it good to keep using the same literary techniques over and over again— or is it?
- Do you think literature makes progress through the centuries, or does its level of artistic achievement remain the same despite technical innovations?
- For decades, writers and critics have been moaning that fiction is on the decline. Do you think it's true?
- What do you think is going to happen next in fiction?

## Chapter 13: How Writers Think

### Chapter Summary

This chapter covers the aspect of writing that's called, in educational parlance, "prewriting"—an inaccurate term, because planning and thinking can and should be carried out at every phase of writing. It can't be stated too often that the pedagogical division of writing into the three stages of prewriting, drafting, and writing is merely an analytic convenience. Writers do all three in every conceivable order and all at once. Planning, for creative writers, is essentially a matter of controlled daydreaming: one sits back and lets one's fantasies proceed. It should be a relaxed, unself-critical activity, but one must at the same time have an eye open for what will be professionally useful. The process is sometimes called " dreaming the scene": summoning up images of one's characters, their actions, and their voices, which one reshapes and translates into language. A writer who engages in this kind of mental activity on a regular basis will get in the habit of being inspired—of achieving a state of intense concentration in which ideas of fiction are most likely to be born. Formal prewriting activities (journals, outlines, etc.) should be made available to students as choices, not duties.

## Approaching the Text

Pointing out that "How do you get your ideas?" is the question most frequently asked of writers, you might ask the same question of students. Allow a free range of techniques of prewriting, both formal and informal, to emerge. (You might wish to list them on the board.) Tell students that the prewriting method this chapter recommends is the least formal of all—easy to understand but requiring discipline and practice to learn effectively.

## Departing from the Text

Every writer, by definition, has his or her own method of finding ideas and planning a story. Nevertheless, it's the case that many writers have described their prewriting techniques as ones of relaxed, self-conscious daydreaming or as a disciplined state of concentration. French literary critic Hélène Cixous, in her essay "Coming to Writing," describes it as "inciting myself: 'Let yourself go, let the writing flow, let yourself steep; bathe, relax, become the river, let everything go, open up, unwind, open the floodgates, let yourself roll...' A practice of the greatest passivity. At once a vocation and a technique...our way—really an active way—of getting to know things by letting ourselves be known by them." You might read this quote aloud as a way of initiating a discussion on students' preferred methods of prewriting. The *Paris Review Writers at Work* series also contains much valuable discussion. Encourage students to discuss the pros and cons of formal versus informal prewriting.

## More Exercises

1. Try automatic writing, a more radical form of freewriting. You simply take a sheet of paper and let your pen write whatever words it wishes to, without thinking at all and without having a topic in mind beforehand. The extent to which you find this valuable is entirely up to you. (Yeats is perhaps the most notable writer to have engaged in long-term automatic writing experiments.)

2.   When planning your next story, reverse your usual prewriting methods: if you currently spend a great deal of time thinking before drafting, cut that time to as little as possible, and if you currently spend very little time thinking before drafting, decide on a period of time that's much longer and force yourself to use up that period before putting a word on paper. If you currently use formal prewriting methods, do without them, and if you currently do without them, choose one or more and use them.

3.   In a paragraph or so, write your own answer to the question, "How do you get your ideas?" Then read your answer, searching for new insights and inspirations that might aid your future prewriting. You may also wish to exchange answers with others.

## Troubleshooting

A key point is to allow as much freedom as possible in prewriting techniques and to encourage students to share their techniques with classmates. If students like to keep their prewriting minimal and go directly to drafting, that too is a perfectly acceptable way of prewriting. If students dislike the pressure that is often exerted in classrooms to use formal prewriting methods, they will find this chapter reassuring. Try to avoid making prewriting into an assignment on its own, a hurdle that must be leaped before the student can begin to put words on paper. Prewriting should liberate rather than inhibit the flow of words.

A problem connected with the practicalities of the course calendar is that there simply may not be enough time to allow every student all the prewriting he or she wishes. If, for example, you're assigning the writing of one short story per month, students who dally in the planning stage may be caught in the third week without having decided on an idea. You can forestall this by holding a prewriting conference with individuals or groups of students perhaps one-fourth of the way toward the deadline for their stories. Students who have done formal prewriting can show it to you at that point; students who haven't should still be able to discuss their progress toward an idea for a story. Point out that while fiction writers ideally can take all the time they need to prewrite, they often do have to work toward a deadline—and that's good discipline in itself.

## Basic Students

Many basic students will be more comfortable with the regularities of formal prewriting than with the total freedom of "dreaming the scene." You'll probably want to provide a considerable amount of informal assessment for such things as journal entries, freewriting notes, and outlines, keeping your comments positive and avoiding any suggestion of grading. Put the emphasis on locating and highlighting those prewriting notes that, in the student's opinion, show most potential for expansion into stories.

## Advanced Students

Some advanced students like to show off how little prewriting they need to do—and that's fine. (You might want to challenge them to try formal prewriting "just to see how the other half lives," though.) Other advanced students might be overscrupulous in making notes and outlines. These students can benefit from being given a time limit or being assigned to do without their usual crutches for at least one story.

## For Discussion

- How important do you feel inspiration is in writing fiction?
- When you read a work of fiction, do you sometimes think you can tell when the writer was inspired and when he or she wasn't? How?
- On the whole, do you think your own writing could benefit from more careful planning—or from less?

# Chapter 14: Necessary Roughness: The First Draft

## Chapter Summary

As with other phases of the writing process, there are as many different methods of writing a first draft as there are writers. Some polish each scene to perfection before going on to the next; others write as fast as possible, heedless of quality, knowing that they'll go back and revise later. As always, the underlying message of this chapter is that the individual writer must find his or her own way of working. The more explicit and specific message is that a rough draft is a place to free oneself from inhibitions, to experiment—often, to exaggerate.

## Approaching the Text

You might take an informal survey of students' methods of drafting. How quickly do they usually write a first draft? How much revision do they usually do in the midst of a rough draft? Do they draft from the beginning of a story to the end or in some other order? Do they tend to work the same way on each story, or does each story call forth its own methods? Point out that any method that works for an individual writer is acceptable, but that the nature of rough drafts makes them particularly suited for a spontaneous, uninhibited approach, allowing the writer to take risks and make mistakes, and that students who have always drafted very carefully in the past may benefit from trying this approach.

## Departing from the Text

This chapter describes a drafting process that holds true for many writers; however, students who have different working methods should be encouraged to talk about them with the class. The idea is not to enforce an orthodoxy, but to make available a pool of possibilities. Anything any writer says about the writing process may unexpectedly provide the crucial turn of the key for some other writer.

## More Exercises

1.  Give yourself a short time limit in which to draft a story—perhaps fifteen minutes per page. Begin with one of the sample opening sentences in exercise 3 on page 149.

2.  With a partner, decide on a short-story premise. Then decide on a page length that you feel is appropriate for the topic. Then have a writing race: at the word "go," each of you writes a story of that length developing that premise. The first person to finish wins. Quality doesn't matter. Read the stories only to make sure that the contestants have stayed on-topic. Then either throw them out or save them for later revision.

3.  During your current work on a story, draft at least two pages without making a single revision. (Of course, you'll probably want to revise those pages in a later draft.)

4.  If your usual method is to begin writing at the beginning of a story and to work straight through till the end, consider trying a different order of battle, beginning at the ending or at some point in the middle. If you don't like that way of working, go back to your old way.

5.  A long-term exercise: Decide on a number of pages, or words, that you will write every day. Stick to your schedule as best you can.

## Troubleshooting

Some students—like many adults—will feel hamstrung by the need to make a given passage perfect before going on to the next one. Try to ascertain whether a student's careful drafting method is constructive or is the product of inhibition. This will take time, because the only way to ascertain it is by reading the results. A student who drafts carefully and emerges with a substantial, well-written work of fiction should be praised. A student who, under the cloak of careful drafting, frets and stalls and emerges with a skimpy product that obviously doesn't fulfill the student's potential, is blocked. (One diagnostic sign of blocking is if later drafts are inferior to the first draft.) Firm deadlines and time-limit exercises like exercise 1, above, may help the blocked student. Self-doubt, perfectionism, and lack of confidence are generally what cause blocks, so your tone in dealing with the student should remain encouraging and confident. Having set a deadline, withdraw so that the student has the freedom and responsibility of drafting his or her own work on schedule; but make yourself available for conferencing at the student's initiative. Students' worries about meeting the deadline should be defused with reassurances, and at times it may be necessary to simply declare a draft finished, telling the student that it's good enough and that no more time should be spent on it. If you feel it's appropriate for a given student, you might recommend relaxation exercises such as visualizing the story for a few minutes before writing or taking ten deep breaths.

## Basic Students

For some students, "drafting" and "writing" will seem synonymous—they won't yet be accustomed to sustained prewriting and revising. Your task with these students is straightforwardly to get them used to the idea that the actual scribbling of words on paper is only one part, and not necessarily the most important part, of writing.

Students who have trouble getting anything at all down on paper might be permitted to dictate their stories into a tape recorder.

## Advanced Students

Some of the brightest students, because they're perfectionistic, may be subject to blocks; for them, see "Troubleshooting" above.

Bright students who enjoy drafting freely can be encouraged to set themselves ambitious goals, such as writing longer works than they've done before or writing a specified (by them) number of pages per day.

## For Discussion

- When reading a work of fiction, have you ever paused at a given passage and thought to yourself, "This is pretty rough; it needs more revision?" Share the experience with the class. Read the passage aloud if possible.

- Does it bother you that a lot of fiction is based on exaggeration and distortion? Why or why not?

- This chapter implies that it doesn't matter very much if a rough draft is of high quality or not, since it will be revised later. Do you agree or disagree? Discuss your reasons.

# Chapter 15: Revising—Or Should I Say Rewriting?

## Chapter Summary

This is one of the longest chapters in the book, reflecting the importance of revision for the writing process. The fundamental message is that every first draft needs to be revised. (The occasional citable exception from great literature does not alter this general truth.) The chapter proposes four levels on which fiction writers revise: diction, scene, structure, and concept. As with prewriting, drafting, and rewriting, these are not mutually exclusive categories: at any given moment, a writer may be revising on one, some, or all four levels. The chapter offers tips for approaching each kind of revision, for determining when more revision is needed, and for knowing when one ought to stop revising.

## Approaching the Text

This is a meaty chapter, and, if you have time, you might want to devote two weeks to it instead of one (or one week instead of half a week—or double whatever your usual time per chapter is). You might begin by asking students how they feel about having to revise drafts of their writing. You're likely to get some negative responses, for writers in general, and young writers in particular, often find revising a burdensome task, in contrast to the freewheeling, inspired mood of drafting. Point out that this is exactly why revision is so important, for the exuberance and enthusiasm of the first draft often give way to doubt and regret when one reads that draft later. The sinking feeling, familiar to innumerable writers when they read their rough work, is a signal that something needs to be fixed—exactly analogous to the physical pain that signals something wrong with our bodies. Fortunately, we can fix our writing by going over it carefully, patiently, slowly—and going over it not just once, but as many times as necessary.

## Departing from the Text

The importance of revision for good writing is widely recognized and really does not admit much debate; student writers who doubt its importance are, in almost all cases, simply mistaken. Just to provide an alternative, you might challenge students to find works that were written with little or no revision. Some, like Faulkner's *As I Lay Dying*, Stendhal's *The Charterhouse of Parma*, and Kerouac's *Visions of Cody*, have been mentioned in the text. Lawrence's *Kangaroo* was written in six weeks. Katherine Anne Porter and William Saroyan sometimes claimed to write their short stories in single sittings. This is not to say that these authors' works could not have been improved by revision. Many is the published work of fiction that would have benefited from another draft. Of course most talented people are *capable* of completing a story-length work quickly, but they really become writers when they realize that isn't enough: there's a big difference between a story-length chunk of fiction and a story. It is conceivable that a genius might not need to revise a given work, but, in the real world, it is not a significant enough possibility to expect; if it ever happens, the writer should look upon it as a happy fluke.

## More Exercises

1. Choose the best material you have written for an exercise in this book. Go back and revise it.
2. Return to a piece of writing you have already revised—and revise it again. Reread it before and after each revision to make sure you haven't made it worse.

## Troubleshooting

Some students, from misplaced pride, may resist the need to revise or may interpret a suggestion to revise as a message that they have done something wrong. There's no instant solution for this, but exposure to a "culture of revision" can help. Talk about revision as a matter-of-fact necessity, part of a job well done, rather than as a burden or a punishment. Praise students who revise effectively. Assign revision as part of the regular course work. Read aloud, or post, comments famous writers have made about the necessity of revision (available in Winokur's *Writers on Writing*, Plimpton's *The Writer's Chapbook*, and elsewhere).

A systemic problem concerning revision in creative writing courses is that there may not be enough time in a semester or two for students to do all the revision they need to. In many creative writing courses, students are asked to hand in one assignment after another in relatively short order and do not have an opportunity to go back to improve a previous draft; as a result, everything handed in is a first draft. The solution is to build revision into your syllabus, as much as time permits. This may mean assigning fewer stories, or fewer pages of fiction, per course. For example, instead of having students turn in four stories, none of which benefit from significant revision, you might have them turn in three, and then, as the final assignment, ask them to choose one of the three and rework it. (A condition of getting a good grade is that they must improve the story!) Or you might require them to revise each story they turn in, after you and the class have commented on it; this produces an alternating schedule of first draft-revision-first draft-revision. One extra week per story for revision is reasonable—more might be preferable but may not be practical for your syllabus.

Even given this kind of schedule, students will probably not get to do as much revising as professional writers would, but they will at least get a taste of revision and learn the necessity for it.

## Basic Students

The big problem for basic students is that they may do a conscientious job of revising a story, and you may see no improvement in its quality—perhaps even a decline in quality—as a result. You might have them revise again with more advanced partners. You might focus on finding the point of diminishing returns in their labors—the point at which, though they may have started out improving the story, they take a downturn; in the future they may be able to sense that point coming. Pacing is likely to be a problem with these students' revisions: they may pad purposelessly or cut past the bone. Encourage them to reread their own work, searching for where it slows down or speeds into hyperdrive. And give credit for effort.

## Advanced Students

Advanced students will enjoy rewriting the works of published writers, both great and not so great.

Some advanced students may be especially resistant to revision on the theory that "I'm so great I get it right the first time." Present revision to them as the hallmark of the true, sophisticated professional. Cite the remark of Thomas Mann (a very great and very methodical writer) that the more he learned about writing, the harder it got for him. Don't worry if they don't buy this message at first—they will when they're older.

## For Discussion

- How do you feel about rewriting? Is there anything you like about it? What do you dislike most about it?

- Why is writing hard?

- In Victorian times, novelists such as Dickens and Trollope often wrote for serial publication, producing a certain number of chapters per monthly issue of a magazine. This meant relatively little time for revision. What were the effects on their work? Why was writing for serial publication easier for them than it would be for a contemporary American? (One modern writer who tried it, as a stunt, was Norman Mailer, in *An American Dream*.)

- The fiction writers today who are most pressured for time are TV writers, especially those who write for daily soap operas. In your opinion, does their work tend to show insufficient revision? How?

- Is there such a thing as too much revision? What are its signs? Cite works you feel have been overrevised.


# Chapter 16: Work Habits, or, Do I Have To?

## Chapter Summary

The chapter poses a fundamental question—"Do I have to write?"—and answers it: "No, but if you want to, you should do it with all your heart, not halfway." The author's personal work habits are described, and famous writers' work habits are mentioned, with the aim of conveying that while no two writers have exactly the same habits, the development of self-discipline is universally desirable. One of the chief results of good work habits, for this author and numerous others, is that the writer acquires the habit of inspiration, learning more easily to enter the concentration state described in Chapter 13.

## Approaching the Chapter

A casual discussion of students' writing habits may be the best way of introducing this chapter. Avoid moralizing when you discuss the importance of good work habits; simply exposing students to the idea is likely to be more effective. Encourage students to share tips on work habits—for example, "I always make a cup of cocoa before I write" or "I write best before nine in the morning." You never know when someone's off-the-cuff remark will provide some future writer with an energizing technique.

## Departing from the Chapter

Self-discipline is desirable in all professions, of course, so you might want to broaden the discussion to include students' work habits in other courses, in after-school jobs, and at sports and hobbies. You're likely to find that students willingly work hardest at the activities that interest them most.

The occasional wiseacre may express doubts about the importance of work habits. Of course, it's possible that a person may only write one thing in his or her life, and that that one thing may become a classic. The person who achieves that, however, has probably developed self-discipline in other walks of life on the way to acquiring the knowledge that went into the writing.

## More Exercises

1.  Envision the work habits that you think would be ideal for a writer. Then try to realize them in your life.
2.  Draw up a writing schedule for at least one week—and keep it.

## Troubleshooting

Poor work habits will show up in the results: in the students' stories. If students submit stories that seem skimpy, ill-planned, marred by careless details or inconsistencies, inadequately proofread, or visually sloppy, you might want to bring up the issues at your conferences. Ask relatively neutral questions such as "How many drafts did you do?" and "How many hours do you estimate this story took to write?" You needn't press the issue or assign students to work harder; that's liable to create resentment, and, after all, students who discover that they don't want to be fiction writers have learned something important.

## Basic Students

Basic students are likely to have work-habit problems in all or most of their courses. You might ask them which courses they're best at and what working techniques they use in those courses; then, if possible, suggest that students adapt those techniques to creative writing. (Students who are good at athletics, shop, music, or domestic science might turn out to have very good work habits in those areas.) You might want to ask these students' other teachers about the strong and weak aspects of their work habits; then try to incorporate the strong points into your own approach.

## Advanced Students

Gifted students, accustomed to finding schoolwork easy, can be susceptible to lazy work habits. Most of the time, the solution is to set the student a greater challenge. In creative-writing terms, this may mean encouraging the student to write something more ambitious—a longer work, for instance. However, quality rather than quantity should be the goal. No matter how precocious a student is, there will be things in his or her work that could be improved by a professional. Look for technical, stylistic, and conceptual weaknesses; point them out in a nice way; discuss possible solutions. This may lead the student to get in the habit of looking for and improving them independently.

## For Discussion

- Do you agree with the author that work habits affect the quality of a writer's creation? Why or why not?

- Can you tell anything about a writer's work habits by reading his or her fiction?

- Imagine two writers who are identical twins. They are both writing stories about the same events in their childhood. (Imagine any event you like, such as a first kiss or the death of a grandparent.) However, one twin writes for three hours every morning, like clockwork, producing three pages a day on the dot; the other twin writes whenever he or she feels like it, in blazing all-night sessions, sometimes two or three nights in a row, and slacks off when he or she isn't in the mood, sometimes going weeks without writing a word. Based on this difference alone, describe any other differences that you imagine will be found in the writers' stories.

## Chapter 17: Audience

### Chapter Summary

This brief chapter investigates the problematic question of how much, or little, to take one's audience into consideration when writing. Many writers, including the author, try to think about the audience as little as possible. Some serious writers, such as John Updike, admit to having in mind an image of an ideal or general reader. But an imagined readership of that kind is merely a projection of one's own feelings: one's projected audience is one's ideal self.

The chapter concludes with a plea against selling out—against pandering to an audience rather than pursuing one's own vision.

### Approaching the Text

Ask students whether or not they write with an audience in mind and whether or not they feel it's a good thing to do so; let them know that this is a debate that has run throughout literary history. To launch the discussion, you might share the following remarks by film journalist David Thomson, from his review of British director Michael Powell's memoir, *Million-Dollar Movie* (reviewed in *The New Republic*, April 25, 1994, p. 41). Powell and his colleague Emeric Pressburger created *The Red Shoes* and many other classic movies. Thomson praises them for resisting pressure from studio executives (who, after all, had wrongly predicted that *The Red Shoes* would never make money). Thomson writes, "I doubt they [Powell and Pressburger] knew or cared 'what the public wanted.' They took that old plea as humbug, and pursued their own fancies. Brooding on the common tastes can be so depressing." Thomson adds that "there's no proven point in *aiming* at the public eye. Aim at your heart, or the mind's eye, and you have as much chance of success as if you calculate the allure of *The Last Action Hero*." Those last two sentences amount to a credo for any artist with a personal vision.

## Departing from the Text

In the author's experience as writer, instructor, and student, serious fiction writers rarely talk about the audience (except for half-facetious complaints that people don't read anymore); in a college creative writing course, the subject is likely to be dismissed as unworthy. Most students, however, have been taught to write with the audience in mind in their high school English courses and their freshman composition courses, where the focus is on nonfiction. The distinction needs to be made. Attention to the audience is most justifiable in persuasive writing, where one is trying to sway readers to a point of view—perhaps even to get their votes or sell them something. In expository writing, it's often useful to have an understanding of the audience's reading level and amount of prior knowledge. And it's important for students who customarily speak colloquially to understand that their essays should be more formal in tone, diction, and sentence structure.

Unfortunately, textbooks that teach the audience-oriented approach to expository writing usually carry it over to creative writing as well. That's largely a matter of fulfilling bureaucratic guidelines: they rarely have much useful, specific advice on aiming one's creative writing at an audience, for the truth is, there is no such good advice.

In writing fiction, one is trying to express oneself and create a work of art. One hopes for an audience, but its claims should not interfere with the claims of one's art and one's spirit, or the result will be hackwork. There are many successful hack writers in this world, but it is not the primary goal of this book to engender them; this book assumes that the reader has a commitment to serious writing, to honest craft. (An assumption which is not literally true of every student, of course; but it is good for students to be treated *as if it were true*. It is a useful fiction.)

The futility of trying to write with an audience in mind is demonstrated by the innumerable movies, books, and TV shows that have been flops despite the most careful targetting, which often involves market surveys and focus groups, and by the low quality of many carefully marketed works that become hits. Consider the following points:

1.  It is extremely difficult to profile one's audience accurately in advance, short of doing a scientific survey. An audience profile before the fact is just a hunch. A work aimed at one segment of the audience may turn out to appeal to a different segment.

2.  Even if one senses who one's audience is, one can't predict how they'll respond to a given work or an aspect of a work—especially given the ever-accelerating

pace of changes in popular trends. One's image of the audience is ultimately an impression in one's own mind, equivalent to one's image of one's acquaintances. How accurately can you tell in advance which books and movies your friends will like—or which ones you yourself will like before you experience them?

3.  In practical terms, addressing the audience almost invariably means writing down to the audience—underestimating them. This means watering down one's vision or one's message; it means self-censorship. It also risks alienating the very people one is trying to reach, since even if they don't share all your knowledge of the subject, they can tell when they're being condescended to. It's insulting to assume that the audience must be catered to with a spoon: that they won't be capable of understanding and appreciating your words if you write exactly the way you want to write, that they only like to hear what they're already used to hearing, and that they don't want to learn what they don't already know.

Those who are concerned about the harmful effects of low expectations on contemporary American education will appreciate this point.

To sum up, an audience may benefit from exposure to an artistic vision they didn't know they were ready for; and if, in the end, they spurn the artist's vision, the artist may find another, more congenial audience instead. Rather than preselecting the audience and tailoring the work to it, the writer should write his or her deepest, truest, best work and trust that it will find some appropriate audience, somewhere, sometime.

## More Exercises

1.  Write a letter to a fiction writer whose work you've enjoyed. Tell the writer what you liked about the work and, tactfully, what you didn't like. Ask the writer for his or her opinion on the question of audience.

2.  Go back to any writing exercise you've done in this course, preferably a brief one, or to a journal entry you've made. Did you write it with a specific audience in mind (your teacher, your classmates)? If so, rewrite it without thinking of an audience at all—thinking only of what you want to say and how best to say it. If not, imagine a specific audience and rewrite the exercise with it in mind.

## Troubleshooting

Good writing can be done with an audience in mind or without one. Accept either position that your students take. If students have previously been expected to write for an audience and feel frustrated or inhibited or confused by that obligation, now is the time to let them know they don't need to.

## Basic Students

As was implied in "Departing from the Text," the main audience problem for basic students comes from substandard or inappropriately colloquial English. (On the other hand, basic students as an audience for their peers' writing are likely to approve of substandard or colloquial English.) Make sure students understand the distinction between appropriate uses of substandard English in fiction (especially in dialogue) and inappropriate uses in most other forms of writing. Put emphasis on the fundamentals of sentence structure, grammar, diction, and proofreading.

## Advanced Students

Some advanced students may relish the opportunity to tweak the audience. Others may prove adept at giving the audience what it wants (the young Sylvia Plath, in her magazine stories, was an example). Try to be generous toward both outlooks.

## For Discussion

- What is artistic integrity?
- What's your opinion on this issue of audience?
- Do you think about an audience while you write, and, if so, what is it?

# Chapter 18: Writer's Ed.

## Chapter Summary

The specific form of education focused on is graduate study for a master of fine arts degree in creative writing. In recent decades, this has become the dominant path to a literary career. The chapter examines the pros and cons of walking this path. The pros: the graduate student becomes part of a community of writers (both professors and fellow students) who provide emotional support and professional contacts; the university provides a setting in which to write and the time to do it in. The cons: graduate education may induce a certain orthodoxy of style and technique; and the workshop experience may or may not actually benefit the student's craft. The chapter recommends that students wait at least a year after graduating from college before entering graduate school; the extra maturity and the material provided by life experience are advantages.

## Approaching the Text

"Let's assume you want to be a professional fiction writer. What do you think would be the best kind of education to prepare you for that?" You might ask students this (or some variation of it) as a springboard to discussing educational strategies. If you're teaching at the college level, your students may be keenly receptive to advice about graduate school. (One tip, by the way, is that a student doesn't have to major in creative writing as an undergraduate to be admitted to a graduate writing program, as long as the student has an impressive writing sample and recommendations from writing instructors.) If you yourself have had graduate school experience—especially if you have attended or have considered attending a creative writing program—by all means share your knowledge. Since some of your students may attend graduate programs in other fields, you may want to widen the discussion, comparing and contrasting the demands, pressures, requirements, satisfactions, and job prospects of, for example, a doctoral program in literature with a master's program in fiction writing.

## Departing from the Text

If you're teaching high school, the subject of graduate school will seem somewhat remote; discuss college education instead. Increasingly, undergraduate students are majoring in creative writing nowadays, but it is still quite possible (and rewarding) for an aspiring writer to enrich his or her education in some other field, taking creative writing as a sideline or minor. Your students are likely to have a wide range of interests and future professional goals. This might be a good point in the course at which to discuss the broader questions of applying to college, selecting a college to go to, and so forth. Point out that it's important to do some research on the academic (and social) strengths and weaknesses of any college one is considering. Sending away for a college catalog is a valuable and easy step. Recommend that students read the section of the catalog that lists faculty and courses in the English or creative writing departments. College guides such as those published by Lovejoy, Barron, and Barnes & Noble may also have useful information, including the national rankings of specific departments.

## More Exercises

1.  Write yourself a letter describing your personal education plan, including alternatives.
2.  Draw up a list of pros and cons for whichever of the following is most imminent for you: attending college; majoring in English; majoring in creative writing; attending graduate school. Consider your list a resource—not an infallible oracle that must be followed. (One big "pro" can often outweigh a dozen little "cons.")
3.  If you're not doing so already, keep a folio of your fiction writing as preparation for sending a sample to colleges or graduate schools you apply to.
4.  Make a point of keeping in touch with anyone you know who is at a more advanced stage of creative writing education than you. Ask that person or persons for advice—but use your critical judgment in assessing the advice.

## Troubleshooting

Depending on their grade level and sophistication, your students may already know a good deal—or nothing at all—about the opportunities available in creative writing education. The overall point to get across is that, from the 1960s to the 1990s, it has become increasingly customary for aspiring writers to pursue at least part of their apprenticeship in a formal university setting rather than by working in isolation, hanging out in cafes, and so forth. Whether this is a healthy phenomenon or not has been much debated, and continues to be debated, but there's no doubt that a degree in creative writing can help one's career.

If you're teaching high school and your students are relatively unsophisticated or come from disadvantaged backgrounds, you should, of course, make every effort to persuade students to stay in school, to attend college—in short, to value educational achievement and to believe that they're capable of it.

## Basic Students

This is tricky, because a student who truly lacks any literary gift should not be encouraged to pursue writing as a career or an academic concentration. However, it's much too early, in high school, to reliably assess the presence or absence of literary talent; and it's easy to mistake a bright-but-bored student for a backward one. These students should be encouraged rather than ignored or discouraged. A seemingly offhand compliment or expression of interest, a casual question about the student's college plans or about the student's tastes in literature and art, may make a difference in his or her life—as can sustained conferences—even if you never learn about the results. Occasionally, a gifted student who does poorly in other courses will shine in creative writing; this kind of student deserves personal attention, positive reinforcement, and steering toward further education that specializes in creative writing. The opportunity to work on a school publication such as a literary magazine may be a lifesaver for such a student; if you can provide that opportunity, do not withhold it on account of a student's poor performance in noncreative-writing courses.

## Advanced Students

As with basic students, the question here is, "Who really belongs in this category?" Students who are generally bright, hardworking, developmentally precocious, and socioeconomically privileged will emerge at the top of your class and should be rewarded with top grades, personal attention, and opportunities to staff the literary magazine (if that's your responsibility). On the other hand, as was indicated above, try not to let those students' virtues blind you to the possible presence of less obvious, but equally strong, potential. Be aware of:

- the student from a background that may not have provided access to books or to the idea of writing as an available, acceptable profession—but who may know things about life that are well worth writing about;
- the shy bookworm who needs drawing-out;
- the student whose developmental schedule is a year or more behind some other students—and who will catch up in adulthood.

If you can't give such students top grades, let them know, in conferences and through casual conversation, that they have minds worth developing, that their grade in your course is not a blanket assessment of their gifts, and that you expect them to move on to higher achievements.

## For Discussion

- How do you see your education progressing over the next few years?
- Based on what you've read (and what you may know from other sources), do you think you'd like to study creative writing at a higher academic level?
- Do you think the increasingly academic environment in which fiction writers find themselves is a healthy development?

# Chapter 19: Careers

## Chapter Summary

Perhaps the most popular career for fiction writers is in teaching creative writing. After discussing pros and cons, the chapter recommends that writers try this option and see whether it suits them. The chapter encourages students to widen their perspective to include other kinds of work, including writing genre fiction for money, writing nonfiction, writing for businesses, educational writing, technical writing, working in publishing, working in journalism and advertising, ghostwriting, and working in non-literary fields.

## Approaching the Text

You'll undoubtedly be studying this chapter late in the course. Like the other chapters in Part Three, it can serve as a coda for the course, perhaps saved for a day when you've cleared away more pressing work, finished discussing student assignments, and are in the mood for a relaxed discussion of students' possible futures. You may want to bring in copies of some of the career guides listed in the "Writer's Bookshelf"; they will prove valuable for students who don't dream of becoming professional writers, as well as those who do.

## Departing from the Text

All your students will be involved in future career decisions, so you needn't limit your discussion of this chapter to careers in writing or careers that will support a writer's life. For instance, you can broaden the discussion of a career as a creative writing teacher to include teaching careers in general. (By all means bring in insights based on your own experiences.) Welcome any input your students have on the subject of careers, especially when it's in the form of practical tips and experiential anecdotes.

## More Exercises

1.  Read any one book listed in the "Writer's Bookshelf" for this chapter and write down at least three things you learn from it that might help you find a job.

2. With a group, brainstorm a list of at least ten jobs *not* mentioned in this chapter that a writer might hold (writing doesn't have to be part of the job itself).

3. Talk to someone whose job you think you might like to hold someday. Ask him or her how to get such a job, what the prerequisites are, and what it's like to work at the job. Report to the class on your interview or invite the interviewee to speak directly to the class.

## Troubleshooting

If the consensus among your students is that they don't yet want to discuss the hard issues of establishing a career, you may skip the subject in class and leave it for one-on-one conferences with those students who are interested.

If there are students in your class who seem keenly interested in pursuing writing careers but who, in your judgment, don't have the potential to make it, try your best *not* to discourage them. They deserve the chance to give it their best shot, and if they fail, they're likely to learn things in the process that will steer them toward their truer callings. And your assessment of their potential may be wrong to begin with, at least to the extent that the student who tries to become a serious writer and fails may end up as a less prestigious but perfectly respectable kind of writer.

## Basic Students

Encourage basic students to keep writing: the skill will help them find jobs in the white-collar technological and service sectors and is valuable for advancement in blue-collar careers as well.

## Advanced Students

Encourage your advanced students to have high goals and to learn as much as they can about the realities of the occupational market while they're still in school. Internships—whether in literary publishing or in other fields of interest, such as politics and journalism—can be a huge boost for the future careers of talented students from diverse backgrounds.

## For Discussion

- What resources are available in your school for finding out about careers?
- What resources are available at the public library?
- What resources are available among people you know and among others in your community whom you could get to know?
- How important do you feel it is to start thinking about careers at your current stage of education? Give reasons for your answer.
- What career ideas do you have that you're willing to share with your peers?

## Chapter 20: Going Public

### Chapter Summary

This chapter deals with publication. Pages 208–212 describe the standard methods of submitting manuscripts to publishers and agents. The role of agents is briefly discussed. The remainder of the chapter discusses what gets published and why. Aside from matters of personal taste, there are three major constraints on editors: time, space, and money. *Time* refers to the extremely limited amount of time editors have in which to read manuscripts by unestablished writers. *Space* refers to the extremely limited number of slots on publishers' lists that are accessible to such writers. *Money* refers to the obligation of editors to turn a profit and to work within a budget. Although the picture is a bleak one, it's mitigated by the fact that there are many publishing houses and little magazines and many editors at each publishing house—in other words, many places to send fiction. The chapter ends by expressing the hope that new technologies such as desktop publishing and the Internet will soon make self-publication a much more available and respectable alternative.

### Approaching the Text

Like Chapter 19, this chapter works best at the end of the course. Ascertain beforehand to what extent your students are seriously interested in getting published someday. Depending on your findings, you may not have to dwell on the subject very long, or you may want to spend an appreciable amount of time—half a class session or more—discussing this chapter.

If any of your students have actually been published, encourage them to share their experiences—likewise if students have submitted works for publication and been turned down.

### Departing from the Text

Many writers feel that apprentice writers nowadays are under too much pressure (sometimes self-inflicted) to publish early. There is little reason for a writer to publish before he or she is ready, and the definition of "ready" is nebulous and variable. There's little to gain from publishing immature work that's ignored or poorly reviewed, earns meager sales, and loses the writer the advantage of making more of a splash with a more mature first publication. Many fine writers deliberately restrain themselves from sending out any but their best work. The point, after all, is to publish work that matters, not just to get one's name in print. Student writers may feel an inner compulsion to get published by the time they graduate from college or by the time they're twenty-five or thirty. Point out that these self-imposed deadlines are arbitrary and unnecessary and have nothing to do with the real place of a writer's development (which is always individual and unpredictable). There are as many different career trajectories as there are writers.

This said, it's still inescapably true that people, especially young people, like to see their work in print and that the most objective test of whether a writer is ready is whether anyone is willing to publish his or her work. We should encourage high standards, but literary monasticism is only for a few.

Give as much guidance as possible to students who are actively seeking publication or planning to. Make sure they know in advance that they are bound to experience frustrations and disappointments but that persistence can overcome this (as can luck and aggressiveness). Steer them toward publications that are relatively realistic goals for students: school literary magazines and commercial and educational magazines that are aimed at their age group. Also recommend self-publishing and alternatives such as founding a literary magazine or writing for science fiction "fanzines." You or your students might establish a series of fiction readings in your community—perhaps at a local bookstore or coffeehouse—if one doesn't already exist.

## More Exercises

1. Give a reading of your work in your class or in a writer's group, over a local access radio or television station, or elsewhere.

2. Hang some of your work up as a poster. (Include a copyright notice.) Get permission to display it in some appropriate local place such as a museum or church.

3. Put together an anthology of your work and your peers'. Distribute copies any way you can think of. Ask your local bookstore to stock copies.

4. Join or form a writers' line on the Internet, and upload a story. (Include a copyright notice and your electronic address or code name, so readers can communicate with you.)

Note: Some instructors assign students to submit stories to magazines, so they'll get a feel for the process. The inevitable result is rejection and hurt feelings; the author does not recommend it.

## Troubleshooting

If your students don't want to discuss publication, you've been saved trouble! If they're keenly interested in the topic, steer them toward books that specialize in it, such as *Applebaum's How to Get Happily Published.* Encourage them to read biographies and interviews to find out how their favorite writers first got published.

An occasional student may have a problem opposite from the one discussed in "Departing from the Text": he or she may have something worthy of publication and not know it. (Most of the time, it will be publication on the student-magazine level.) Such students need ego-boosting in the form of praise and suggestions. Even the simple comment, "I think you might be able to get this published somewhere," is likely to be a longed-for surprise for the student. Do some research so that you can recommend appropriate publication outlets; persist, persuade, and be willing to handle the student's manuscript submission process yourself, perhaps with a letter of recommendation.

## Basic Students

No student is too basic to self-publish. An anthology of a whole class' work is a particularly attractive form for basic students.

## Advanced Students

Encourage the long-term goals of advanced students, but let them know that, no matter how gifted they are, they must be willing to exercise patience and put up with setbacks. (This process, in itself, can be a valuable spur to maturation for the young and gifted.) It's fine if they dream of publishing their first novel, but they should be aware that any novel they write while still in school is very unlikely to get published—but that it's worth writing anyway, as training.

## For Discussion

- What was your image of the publishing world before you read this chapter? How did this chapter change that image?
- Did reading this chapter encourage you to want to become a published writer? Discourage you? Both? Explain.
- What do you think the future of the publishing industry is going to be?
- Read the most recent issues of *Publishers Weekly*, *Poets and Writers*, and *Writer's Digest* magazines. Discuss.
- Based on what you know so far, what do you think it takes for a writer to get published?

# Chapter 21: Living

## Chapter Summary

The writer's life is one of freedom and personal growth; it is also one of frustration and rejection. Balancing these conditions is part of every writer's lifework and, in fact, contributes to personal growth.

The chapter asks two time-honored questions: (1) "Do you have to suffer to sing the blues?" Do writers need to suffer more than other people? No—especially since suffering is involved in the process of becoming a writer itself. What writers need to do is to be more aware of suffering (as of every other human experience) than the average person. (2) "Am I talented?" This is dismissed as a question the student needn't ask about himself or herself. If talent does exist, its presence can be demonstrated only after a writer's work has been accomplished. It should not be used as a precondition to writing, because many factors other than talent go into success, and because opinions about one's talent can be wrong.

The chapter's two-sentence final paragraph, combined with the first sentence of the "Introduction", form a logical syllogism that encloses the entire book in a loop:

A writer is someone who is always learning to write.

A writer is someone for whom living and writing are the same thing.

Therefore, a writer is someone who is always learning to live.

## Approaching the Text

This chapter is intended as a thought-provoking wrap-up to the course, a pointer toward the student's future, and a discussion of the current state of writing in America. You might introduce it by asking students to describe their visions of how a writer lives. The typical nonprofessional's image of a writer's life is accurate on some points but distorted on others. All your students' answers, however, may be interesting fictions!

## Departing from the Text

The chapter concludes on a philosophical note, and by no means is it expected that all writers and all readers will agree with the author's opinions. The fact that those opinions have been expressed, however, highlights once again the book's function as a model of personal writing. Encourage students to discuss, or write about, their own visions of what it means to be a writer.

## More Exercises

1. Write a short story about a writer who is rich and famous.

2. Write a short story about a writer who is poor and unknown. (Exercises 1 and 2 can be combined into one story.)

3. If you have done exercises 1 and/or 2, to what extent do you think your stories show the truth about the writing life, and to what extent do you think they're fabrications or distortions?

4. Read biographies, memoirs, or interviews with several writers. What do they tell you about the writing life?

5. Write a letter to an author you respect, asking him or her for an opinion on whether young people should try to become writers. With a group of classmates, amass a file of responses.

6. If there are published fiction writers in your community (and there probably are), invite them to talk to your class about their lives, their careers, and their work.

## Troubleshooting

Students who are not fairly knowledgeable about current literature may not be interested in the critical content of the chapter's concluding pages. These issues can be treated as a sidelight. Most students will probably be more interested in the issues discussed in the "Chapter Summary": the questions of talent, of suffering, and of personal freedom.

Some students may feel that the chapter's view of the writing life is excessively pragmatic. It is not. It is realistic. Every way of life has its own difficulties, and this book tries to set forth those of a writer's life. Leading starry-eyed aspirants down the primrose path is not an aim of this book, nor is it necessary, as part of a creative writing course, to persuade students that fiction writing is a fun pastime. Fiction writing provides real gratifications that go far deeper than fun—the gratifications of successful struggle, gradual mastery, and continuous self-discovery. Aspiring writers who have a true calling will not be discouraged by this presentation; they will be armed and inspired by its realism. If some students, based on this description of the writing life, decide it's not for them, that in itself is a service a creative writing course can perform, as students go on to find their identities and shape their goals.

## Basic Students

You might ask basic students to write, or state aloud, brief summaries of the positive and negative points this chapter makes about the writing life; or have basic students discuss the topic with more advanced partners. Encourage students to compare and contrast these points with positive and negative points that could be made about other careers.

## Advanced Students

Encourage advanced students to read literary biographies in order to become acquainted with great writers and their lives and to read book reviews in order to become acquainted with the current literary scene.

## For Discussion

- What, in your opinion, is the essential message of this chapter? What are the major themes of this book?

- Name some writers you're familiar with who, in your opinion, had good lives. Name some who had bad lives.

- Based on what you know at this point, do you think you would enjoy being a writer? Why or why not?

- What have you learned from this book about the craft of writing? About practical matters such as getting published? About more intangible matters?

- What would you like to learn about writing that this book hasn't taught you? How do you think you could go about learning it?

# Bibliography

Selected books and articles of particular interest to teachers of creative writing.

## Books

Bernays, Anne, and Pamela Painter. *What If?: Writing Exercises for Fiction Writers.* New York: Harper, 1990. Many of the exercises are adaptable for classroom use.

Berthoff, Ann E. *The Making of Meaning: Metaphors, Models, and Maxims for Writing Teachers.* Portsmouth, NH: Boynton Cook, 1991. Berthoff's aim, here and in all her work, is to make the writing class a setting for intellectual discovery. Her concentration is on nonfiction composition, but all writing teachers should find passages that will inspire them. This book includes provocative quotations and essays by thinkers such as William James, Charles Sanders Peirce, Alfred North Whitehead, Maria Montessori, and Leo Tolstoy.

---, ed. *Reclaiming the Imagination: Philosophical Perspectives for Writers and Teachers of Writing.* Portsmouth, NH: Boynton Cook, 1984. Further insights on Berthoff's vision of literary composition as an activity of the imaginative mind, a form of knowing. Fifty essays by artists and critics such as Paul Klée, Paul Cézanne, Walker Percy, Suzanne K. Langer, Samuel Taylor Coleridge, E. H. Gombrich, and I. A. Richards.

Calkins, Lucy McCormick. *The Art of Teaching Writing.* Portsmouth, NH: Heinemann, 1984. Significant updating of a well-known, well-written handbook on turning the classroom into a writers' workshop, by the founding director of the Teachers College Writing Project.

Harris, Muriel. *Teaching One-to-One: The Writing Conference.* Urbana, IL: National Council of Teachers of English, 1986. A plea for making the conference a major teaching tool, and a practical guide to doing so.

Koch, Kenneth. *Wishes, Lies, and Dreams.* New York: Vintage, 1970. The classic on Koch's experiences teaching the students of P.S. 61, Manhattan, to write poetry.

---. *Rose, Where Did You Get that Red?* Rev. ed. New York: Vintage, 1990. The equally classic sequel to *Wishes, Lies, and Dreams,* with a new afterword for teachers.

Lane, Barry. *After THE END: Teaching and Learning Creative Revision.* Portsmouth, NH: Heinemann, 1993. Using mini-lessons to get students to enjoy and appreciate revision.

Lopate, Phillip. *Being with Children.* New York: Doubleday, 1975; Poseidon, 1989. One writer's reflections on his experiences teaching writing in schools.

---, ed. *Journal of a Living Experiment: A Documentary History of the First Ten Years of Teachers & Writers Collaborative.* New York: Teachers & Writers

Collaborative, 1979. Includes commentary by Lopate, a central figure in the Collaborative, and other participants.

Macrorie, Ken. *Telling Writing*. 2nd ed. Hayden, 1976. A refreshing, readable guide that tries to reinstate truthtelling and liveliness into the writing curriculum—and practices what it preaches.

Mohr, Marian M. *Revision: The Rhythm of Meaning*. Portsmouth, NH: Boynton Cook, 1984. How to help students improve their drafts. Focuses on nonfiction composition.

Romano, Tom. *Clearing the Way: Working with Teenage Writers*. Portsmouth, NH: Heinemann, 1987. Likable description of how one writing teacher learned his craft.

Rose, Mike. *Lives on the Boundary*. New York: Penguin, 1989. A sympathetic view of remedial students by a writer who was one himself.

Shaughnessy, M. P. *Errors and Expectations: A Guide for the Teacher of Basic Writing*. Oxford: Oxford UP, 1977. Useful for teachers of basic or blocked students.

Sottlar, James, ed. *Teaching the Gifted*. Urbana, IL: National Council of Teachers of English, 1988. Contains material on identifying talented student writers and creating individualized instruction for them.

Washton, Andrew D. *What Happens Next? Stories to Finish for Intermediate Writers*. New York: Teachers College Press, 1978. Forty story beginnings. Aimed at middle school, but many of the stories are usable for older adolescents.

Willis, Meredith Sue. *Personal Fiction Writing: A Guide for Writing from Real Life for Teachers, Students, and Writers*. New York: Teachers & Writers Collaborative, 1984. Focuses mostly on elementary and middle-school writing, but is intended to be adaptable for higher levels as well. Many specific assignments, plus examples of student writings.

---. *Deep Revision: A Guide for Teachers, Students, and Other Writers*. New York: Teachers & Writers Collaborative, 1993. Again spans the grade levels. Chapter Seven focuses on fiction.

Ziegler, Alan. *The Writing Workshop*. New York: Teachers & Writers Collaborative, Vol. 1, 1981; Vol. 2, 1984. Volume 1 sets forth a workshop method; volume 2 enumerates assignments and supplies sample student work with instructor comments.

## Articles

Emanuel, Lynn. "In Praise of Malice: Thoughts on Revision." *AWP Chronicle* (Sept. 1991). A much-needed, iconoclastic warning against excessive revision.

Sullivan, Patrick. "Responding to Student Writing: The Consequences of Some Common Remarks." *English Journal* 75 (Feb. 1986). Analyzes frequent teacher comments and how students interpret them.